The National Theatre
The Abbey and Peacock Theatres

Made in
China

by Mar

GW00597479

The National Theatre gratefully acknowledges the financial
support from the Arts Council/An Chomhairle Ealaíon

The Arts Council
An Chomhairle Ealaíon

Made in China

by Mark O'Rowe

Made in China by Mark O'Rowe was first performed at the Peacock Theatre, Dublin on 5 April 20
Press Night was 10 April 2001.

There will be one interval of 15 minutes

Paddy	Luke Griffin
Hughie	Anthony Brophy
Kilby	Andrew Connolly
Director	Gerard Stembridge
Designer	Bláithín Sheerin
Costume Designer	Eimer Ní Mhaoldomhnaigh
Lighting Designer	Ben Ormerod
Fight/Movement Director	Mikel Murfi
Martial Arts Advisor	Maurice Joyce
Sound	Cormac Carroll
Stage Director	Audrey Hession
Assistant Stage Manager	Maree Kearns
Voice Coach	Andrea Ainsworth
Set	Abbey Theatre Workshop
Costumes	Abbey Theatre Wardrobe Department

Please note that the text of the play which appears in this volume may be changed
ing the rehearsal process and appear in a slightly altered form in performance.

ark O'Rowe *Author*

ark was born in Dublin in 1970. Previous plays include **From Both Hips** (Fishamble
eatre Company), **Anna's Ankle** (Bedrock Productions) and **Howie the Rookie** which won
e George Devine Award, the Rooney Prize for Irish Literature and the Irish Times/ESB
vard for Best Play.

erard Stembridge *Director*

erard Stembridge has worked extensively in Dublin theatre both writing and directing.
e has also written and directed for radio, television and film. This is his first production
the National Theatre since **The Comedy of Errors** (1993). He has been a fan of Mark
Rowe's work since he judged a first-time writers competition for NAYD and Mark's play
e **Aspidistra Code** emerged as one of the winners. Gerard directed a public reading of
on the Peacock Stage.

áithín Sheerin *Designer*

áithín trained in sculpture and performance art at NCAD and in theatre design at Motley
Riverside Studios, London. Previous work at the Abbey and Peacock Theatres includes
en, **As the Beast Sleeps** and **You Can't Take it with You**. She was Design Consultant on
ice's Adventures in Wonderland/Alice Through the Looking Glass, Blue Raincoat/Peacock
rtners. Other designs include **The Comedy of Errors**, RSC, **Our Father**, Almeida Theatre,
e **Importance of Being Earnest**, West Yorkshire Playhouse, **Juno and the Paycock**, Lyric
eatre, **The Beckett Festival** (composite set design), Gate Theatre, John Jay Theatre, New
rk. She has also designed for Druid, Groundwork, Charabanc, Red Kettle, TEAM, Second
ce, Fishamble, Galloglass and Prime Cut theatre companies. Her designs for Rough Magic
eatre Company include **The Whisperers**, **The School for Scandal**, **Northern Star**,
ntecost, **The Way of the World**, **The Dogs**, **Digging for Fire** and **Love and a Bottle**.
ntecost was performed at The Kennedy Center, Washington as part of the Island: Arts
m Ireland Festival, May 2000. Most recently she designed **The Fourth Wise Man** at the
k.

ner Ní Mhaoldomhnaigh *Costume Designer*

ner is a graduate of the Limerick School of Art and Design. After a period spent working
the fashion industry in Madrid she returned to Ireland in the early 90's and has since
en working as a costume designer, mainly in film and television. Her credits include
ack Day at Black Rock, **Rebel Heart**, **The Most Fertile Man in Ireland**, **Socks**, **Lives and
deotape**, **The Story of Majella McGinty**, **About Adam**, **Mad about Mambo**, **The
bassador** and **Gold in the Streets**.

Ben Ormerod *Lighting Designer*

Ben's extensive theatre credits include **The House, The Wake, The Colleen Bawn** and **The Freedom of the City** Abbey and Peacock Theatres, **The Leenane Trilogy** including **The Beauty Queen of Leenane** which transferred to Broadway (Druid Theatre Company/Royal Court), **The Country Boy,** Druid Theatre Company, **The Winter's Tale, Uncle Vanya, Accidental Death of an Anarchist Bent** and Pinter's new adaptation of **A la Recherche du Temp Perdu** at the Royal National Theatre, **The Revenger's Tragedy, Two Gentlemen of Verona** and **Henry V** RSC, **Roots, Hamlet** and **Twelfth Night,** Oxford Stage Company, **The Seagull, Hamlet** and **Hedda Gabler,** English Touring Theatre/Donmar Warehouse, **Pera Palas,** Gate Theatre, **Death of a Salesman,** Birmingham Rep, **Twelfth Night** and **Rose Rage,** Watermill Theatre, **The Masterbuilder** English Touring Theatre, **God's Plenty,** Rambert Dance Company and **See Blue Through,** Ballet Gulbenkian. Opera credits include **The Wild Man** and **Punch and Judy,** Aldeburgh Festival, **Baa Baa Black Sheep,** Opera North /BBC 2, **The Mask of Orpheus,** Royal Festival Hall, **Cosi Fan Tutte** and **Il Trovatore,** Scottish Opera, **The Cunning Peasant** and **La Fedelta Premiata,** Guildhall, **Beatrice Cenci,** Spitalfields Opera and **The Coronation of Poppea,** The Purcell Quartet, Japan. Forthcoming work includes **Julius Caesar,** RSC, **A Streetcar Named Desire,** Northern Ballet Theatre and **The Father,** Contemporary Theatre of Athens.

Mikel Murfi *Fight Director*

Mikel is from Sligo. He trained at Ecole Jacques Lecoq, Paris and returned there in 1995 to take the third year pedagogical degree. Previous work at the Abbey and Peacock Theatres includes **The Tempest** and **The Comedy of Errors**. He was a founding member of Barabbas....the company. He directed **Diamonds in the Soil** and **The Lost Days of Ollie Deasy** for Macnas. Mikel has worked with Druid, Passion Machine, Pigsback and Rough Magic theatre companies. Films include **The Commitments, Guiltrip, The Butcher Boy, Sweety Barrett, Love and Rage, The Last September** and **The Three Joes**. Writing and performing work for Irish television includes **Nothing to It, Ten Minute Tales** and **Den 2**.

Anthony Brophy *Hughie*

Anthony's previous work for the Abbey and Peacock Theatres includes **Barbaric Comedies** and **Twenty Grand**. Other theatre credits include **The Lonesome West,** Royal Court Theatre, London, **Shoot the Crow, The Blue Macushla,** Druid Theatre Company, **Sexual Perversity in Chicago,** Players Theatre, **The Illusion,** Charabanc Theatre Company, **Hamlet, Don Juan,** Project Arts Centre, **The Plough and the Stars,** Second Age Theatre Company, **Studs** for Passion Machine, Edinburgh and Liverpool Playhouse, **Tangles,** Project Arts Centre and Royal National Theatre, London. On radio he was a regular character in **Overrun,** RTE. Television and film credits include **Making the Cut, Ballykissangel, The Governor, Razor, Rebel Heart, Ordinary Decent Criminal, The Last Bus Home, The Devils Own, Some Mothers Son, The Informant, Snow White in the Black Forest, Nothing Personal, Run of the Country, In the Name of the Father** and **The Bargain Shop.**

Andrew Connolly *Kilby*

Andrew's last appearance at the Abbey and Peacock Theatres was in **The Lower Depths.** Other theatre work includes **Studs, Wasters, Drowning, Pilgrims** and **War** with Passion Machine, **The Silver Tassie** and **Night Shade** with Rough Magic Theatre Company. Television credits include **Rebel Heart, Taggart, Making the Cut, Bramwell, Circle of Deceit, Troubles, The Truth about Clare, The Bill** and **Lovejoy.** Films include **Vendetta, The Hunted, Cast a Cold Eye, Guiltrip** (for which he was voted Best Actor at the 1995 Amiens Film Festival), **Mad Dogs and Englishmen, Runway One, The Family, The Wolves The Howling, Patriot Games, Joyriders** and **The Courier.**

Mike Griffin *Paddy*

Mike's previous work with the Abbey and Peacock Theatres includes **On the Outside, Overlands, Drama at Inish** and **Moving.** Other theatre work includes **Borstal Boy** and **Juno and the Paycock** at the Gaiety Theatre. Television credits include **Band of Brothers, Vicious Circle, The Ambassador, The Governor** and **Ballykissangel.** Films include **Borstal Boy, Durango, Cast a Cold Eye, Michael Collins, The Nephew** and **The Disappearance of Finbar.**

Amharclann Na Mainistreach
The National Theatre

Sponsors
Aer Lingus
Anglo Irish Bank
Ferndale Films
Dr. A. J. F. O'Reilly
RTE
Smurfit Ireland Ltd
TDI Metro Ltd
The Irish Times

Benefactors
Aer Rianta
AIB Group
An Post
Behaviour and Attitudes
eircom
Electricity Supply Board
Independent News and Media plc
Irish Life & Permanent plc
IIB Bank
Merc Partners
John & Viola O'Connor
Pfizer International Bank Europe
Scottish Provident Ireland
SDS
SIPTU
Unilever Ireland plc
VHI

Patrons
J. G. Corry
Brian Friel
Guinness Ireland Group
Irish Actors Equity
Gerard Kelly & Co
Mercer Ltd
Smurfit Corrugated Cases
Sumitomo Finance (Dublin)
Total Print and Design
Francis Wintle

Sponsors of the
National Theatre Archive
Jane & James O'Donoghue
Sarah & Michael O'Reilly
Rachel & Victor Treacy

Friends of the Abbey
Mr. Ron Bolger
Mr. Joseph Byrne
Ms. Zita Byrne
Lilian & Robert Chambers
Ms. Orla Cleary
Ms. Patricia Devlin
Paul & Florence Flynn
Ms. Christina Goldrick
Mrs. Rosaleen Hardiman
Sean & Mary Holahan
Mrs. Madeleine Humphreys
Ms. Eileen Jackson
Ms. Kate Kavanagh
Mr. Francis Keenan
Vivienne & Kieran Kelly
Joan & Michael Keogh
Mr. Brian Kettle
Donal & Máire Lowry
Mr. Fechin Maher
McCann FitzGerald Solicitors
Ms. Gill McCullough
Mr. Joseph McCullough
Marcella & Aidan McDonnell
Mr. Liam MacNamara
Mr. Chris Morash
Mr. Donal O'Buachalla
Mr. Vincent O'Doherty
Mr. Andrew Parkes
Mr. Terry Patmore
Dr. Colette Pegum
Mr. Michael P. Quinn
Fr. Frank Stafford

Amharclann Na Mainistreach
The National Theatre

The National Theatre
The Abbey and Peacock Theatres

Since its formation as the National Theatre of Ireland
by W B Yeats and Lady Augusta Gregory in 1904,
the Abbey Theatre has been the cradle of new
drama in Ireland for successive generations of
Irish playwrights. From the early works of Synge
and O'Casey, through to those writers at the cutting
edge of Irish theatre today, new plays have remained
at the very core of the Abbey's artistic policy and
have helped to establish and maintain its reputation
as Ireland's foremost cultural institution.

MADE IN CHINA
Mark O'Rowe

Characters
HUGHIE
PADDIE
KILBY

ACT ONE

Lights down. Buzzing. Lights up to reveal an apartment, front door right, door to kitchen, left, window at back. Buzzing. HUGHIE enters from kitchen, goes to window, looks out/down. Goes over to front door, pushes button on intercom.

HUGHIE (*into speaker*). Yeah?

PADDY (*through speaker*). You right, man?!

    HUGHIE *buzzes him in, puts the front door on the latch, exits to kitchen. Pause. PADDY enters, soaking wet, wearing a snorkel jacket, zipped right up, hiding his face. Looks around him, tries to zip down his hood.*

HUGHIE (*popping his head into the room*). What's the jack, man?

PADDY. Fuckin' hell!

HUGHIE. Bit of bad, yeah?

    HUGHIE *disappears again. PADDY continues at the hood. HUGHIE returns with a towel.*

    Out the other day, I was, an' . . . Give us a shot. (*Attempting to open* PADDY*'s zip.*) Was out the other day, man . . . (*Hurting his finger.*) Ouch! (*Attempting again.*) . . . Right? an' . . . (*Of finger.*) Agh! (*Giving up.*) You're gonna have to lift it over your head.

    PADDY *lifts snorkel over head.*

    What was I . . . ?

    PADDY *hands snorkel to him.*

    Hunky. Fuck was I sayin'?

PADDY. You were out.

HUGHIE. That's right. . . . Heavens opened an' I nearly wept. Faggot an' all, I know, but it just set me off. Frustration, disappointment . . .

PADDY. . . . wet . . .

HUGHIE. . . . wet, man. Oppression . . . (*Hanging up snorkel.*) The fuck happened this?

There is a huge rip down the side.

PADDY. Wait an' I tell you . . .

HUGHIE. Nasty!

PADDY. . . . Yeah, moseyin' up Pike Avenue, I was an' . . .

HUGHIE. This tonight?

PADDY. . . . Me way over. An' your man, that fat fuck copper. Dolan, is it? Beset me, the fuck, fucked me in a puddle . . .

HUGHIE. *Beset* you?!

PADDY. Came out of nowhere. Yep. Riefed me bod sneaky an' sent me fuckin' flyin'.

HUGHIE. An' what'd he say?

PADDY. Said nothin', man. Swaggered off, left me all prostrate in the gutter. (*Beat.*) Guffawed.

HUGHIE *does Dolan's laugh.*

Hmm.

HUGHIE. No?

PADDY *does Dolan's laugh.*

Not bad. Not bad . . .

PADDY. Cheers.

HUGHIE. . . . Not *great,* now.

PADDY. Me fuckin' snorkel. (*Pause.*)

HUGHIE. Say he saw you with meself, man.

PADDY. Say so?

HUGHIE. . . . thought you were an echelon. Say he confused you.

PADDY. But I thought with the treaty an' all, he couldn't go near youse.

HUGHIE. Well, where'd it happen? What'd you say, Pike Avenue? You see? That's outside . . .

PADDY. I see. Puppacat's . . .

HUGHIE (*simultaneous with 'puppacat's'*). . . . Puppacat's
boundaries, yeah. Echelons go outside those, man, it's
watch your fuckin' hoop. Treaty doesn't exist past the
Bannerman Flush, so for future reference, occurs again, man,
don't speak, don't look at him. Not that you *did*, but . . .

PADDY. No, but don't give him a reason.

HUGHIE. This is it, man. 'Cos that's all he wants.

PADDY. Right. Reason to smack you.

HUGHIE. Smack or arrest you, the fuck!

PADDY (*pause*). Might be time to put it out to pasture.

HUGHIE. Mmm. Which?

PADDY. Snorkel.

HUGHIE. Might *be*. You gonna get a new one?

PADDY. Might *do*. Or somethin' else, maybe.

HUGHIE. Get somethin' looks well. Not that your snorkel
didn't.

PADDY. No.

HUGHIE. . . . But it didn't. Have to say, now. You want, I'll
come with you.

PADDY. Will you?

HUGHIE. Give you a hand, sure. We pop down to Poppin'
Mossey's an' peruse relaxed, yeah? Take our time an' see
what we can . . . (*Jumps suddenly.*) *Fuck* . . . in' hell!

PADDY. What . . . ?

HUGHIE (*fiddling at his hip*). *Fuck* . . . in'beeper. (*Gets it
turned off.*) Have it on the hummin' thing, I do. You know
the hummin' thing?

PADDY. The *vibratin'* thing.

HUGHIE (*looking at beeper*). Frightened the muck out of me.
(*Of number.*) Kilby.

PADDY. Show?

HUGHIE (*handing it to him*). Fuck does *he* want? Got it down the windsor market.

PADDY. No mobiles, no?

HUGHIE. I wouldn't *get* a mobile, Paddy. Give meself skull cancer, all that? *Fuck* that. Fuckin' brain carbuncles?

PADDY. Brain what?

HUGHIE. Carbuncles, man. That's what you get. Dirty warts on the fucker. Anyway, the bloke told us Pacino uses the same one in that film 'Heat'. You know it?

PADDY. Plays the copper.

HUGHIE. Same as Pacino's, he says. I tells Kilby, you know what Kilby says?

PADDY. What?

HUGHIE. Is that a karate film?

PADDY. You're jokin'!

HUGHIE. Karate film with fuckin' Al Pacino!

PADDY. You're gonna ring him back?

HUGHIE. Fuckim, he thinks I'm goin' out in that, he can suck me . . . (*Bends forward suddenly, holds stomach, in pain.*)

PADDY. You all right, man?

HUGHIE. Fuckin' belly's seizin' up. (*Continues to wince, bent forward, then relaxes a little, sits back.*) Fuckin' hell.

PADDY. What's it? D'you want somethin'?

HUGHIE. Fuckin' pissed-off-ness, man. No thanks. Feels like, you know your grill gets dirty? Every so often a lump of grease . . . You know that?

PADDY. Yeah.

HUGHIE. . . . Explodes? Pops up?

PADDY. I know it.

HUGHIE. Like that. Scalds the fuckin' belly off me. (*Short pause.*)

PADDY. What d'you mean 'pissed-off-ness?'

HUGHIE. With it all, Paddy; with *them* all, fuckin' . . .

PADDY. People, is it?

HUGHIE. *Cunts*, man. Not people. Dirty rotten . . . Excludin' yourself. Yourself an' meself.

PADDY. Right.

HUGHIE. . . . *Cunts,* they are! (*Pause.*)

PADDY. Is it your oul'one? Don't wanna . . .

HUGHIE. No. What *happened* me oul' one?

PADDY. Yeah. Don't wanna be . . .

HUGHIE. *No*, man. She'd be exempt as well, by the way.

PADDY. Right. Well, *course* she would. 'Course, an' how is she?

HUGHIE (*looks at him*). 'Fere not to . . .

PADDY. Fine.

HUGHIE. You mind? Bit fuckin' distressin'.

PADDY. I understand, man. (*Standing up, picking at his trousers.*) You all right now?

HUGHIE. What're you doin'? Yeah, I'm grand.

PADDY. Pants're stickin' to me.

HUGHIE. Pants?

PADDY. Yeah.

HUGHIE. Your *trou*sers.

PADDY (*going over to the radiator, feeling it*). The scaldie stomach of stress, you have. That it?

HUGHIE. That's fuckin' it, man.

HUGHIE *exits.* PADDY *begins taking his trousers off.*
HUGHIE *re-enters.*

Fuck're you doin'?

PADDY. Don't wanna be sittin' in wet all night. D'you mind? (*Hanging trousers over the radiator.*) Me upper body's dry, like, protection of me snorkel an' all. It's just me bottom half.

HUGHIE. What about a new pair? Kettle's on, by the way. Go with the jacket, like. No? Or a shirt somethin' like this, product of John Rocha. You know John? Looks like your man out of 'One Flew Over The Cuckoo's Nest,' the Chief.

PADDY. He an Indian?

HUGHIE. 'Course he is. (*Short pause.*) The chief?

PADDY. No, your man. The bloke you're . . .

HUGHIE. *Ah*, no. Irish, man. Far's I know. So, what d'you think?

PADDY (*going over to snorkel*). Think a new jacket's about as far's I'm willin' to go, man. For the moment, anyway. Say the kettle's on?

HUGHIE. I did, yeah.

PADDY. Sage, man. So . . . (*Taking a video tape from snorkel pocket.*) 'Big Boss?' (*Sitting back down.*) Or 'Eight Diagram Pole Fighters?' Which one d'you wanna go? Good double.

HUGHIE. It is, but . . .

PADDY. *Excellent* double. Distract you from your woes, man.

HUGHIE. . . . Bit of bad news, Paddy. Don't think we're gonna be able to go either. Have to split after.

PADDY. Out?

HUGHIE. Have to do some stuff. (*Beat.*) Regrets, man.

PADDY. Ah, now, you could've *told* me, Hughie. Jaysus.

HUGHIE. I know.

PADDY. Went down the phone box, an' . . .

HUGHIE. . . . The rain, but . . .

PADDY. . . . an' gave me a ring at least. *I* came down in the rain.

HUGHIE. But you'd your snorkel, Paddy.

PADDY. Ah, now, lay off the fuckin' snorkel, will you? Come on.

HUGHIE. All right. Regrets.

PADDY. So, d'you want me to head? Or . . .

HUGHIE. Ah no, sure we've an hour or so. What about that?
D'you wanna hang around for . . . ?

PADDY. Sure, fuck it. Have to wait 'til me pants dry a bit,
anyway. So, c'mere . . .

HUGHIE. There's . . . *Pants?!*

PADDY. *Trousers*, fucksake! Whatever!

HUGHIE. There's the kettle, now.

They stare at each other. Long pause. PADDY *exits to the
kitchen. Pause.*

Got this killer headache yesterday mornin'. Thought it was
a tumour I developed or somethin', come from all the bile
I've been buildin' up.

Over following, PADDY *in and out of kitchen doing tea
business.*

PADDY. 'Count of what?

HUGHIE. Huh . . . ?

PADDY. Why were you buildin' up bile?

HUGHIE. 'Count of cunts, man.

PADDY. I *know* cunts. Who?

HUGHIE. Puppacat. (*Pause.*) Fuck askin' me to do some
business tonight. 'Bit of business, Hughie.' Like that. On'y
not askin' . . .

PADDY. Right. Tellin'.

HUGHIE (*simultaneous with 'tellin''*). Fuckin' tellin'. Which is
why we can't watch the flick, man. (*Pause, sips tea.*)

PADDY *turns his trousers over.*

Still. This is what comes of bein' an echelon.

PADDY. Downsides?

HUGHIE. *An* up, man. Like an'thin'. You don't deserve the
rewards you reap if you're not prepared to toil.

PADDY (*looking out window*). An' you do reap, man. You
can't deny. Your threads, this pad . . .

HUGHIE. I'm not denyin'.

PADDY. You're just complainin', that it?

HUGHIE. 'Zactly, man. Just havin' an oul' moan, I am. (*Pause.*) Eh, Paddy.

PADDY. What? Oh. (*Puts his flute away. Sitting down.*) So, what's he want you to do, man?

HUGHIE. You know Bernie Denk? (*Pause.*) You *do*, man. Green boots, got the little moustache, there . . .

PADDY. *Oh*, yeah. Yeah . . .

HUGHIE. . . . the duffel . . .

PADDY. . . . I know him. What d'you think of that duffel?

HUGHIE. *Muck*, man. You thinkin' of gettin' one?!

PADDY. Well . . .

HUGHIE. Fuck *that*, Paddy. There's more style in your snorkel. Fuck was I?

PADDY. Is he the one got up on his oul'one?

HUGHIE. They *say*.

PADDY. . . . They say got up on his oul'one?

HUGHIE. That's him. Fuckin' Puppa wants me to break his pins.

PADDY. Hmm. (*Pause.*) See the problem there's . . .

HUGHIE. It's not fuckin' appropriate.

PADDY. Well, it's not the 'propriate *time*, man.

HUGHIE. That's, yeah.

PADDY. . . . You know? For *you*.

HUGHIE. Well, that's what I *mean*, man. (*Pause.*)

PADDY. Do *you* think he got up on her?

HUGHIE (*jumps in fright*). Bollox! (*Checks his pager.*) Fuckhead again, for fuck sake. I don't see why he can't be the one goes up, does it stead of annoyin' me all fuckin' night, permy cocksucker *like* him. I'm puttin' that on beep. (*He pushes buttons and the pager beeps.*) Hear that?

PADDY. Is he?

HUGHIE. What?

PADDY. A cocksucker. I *did* hear it.

HUGHIE. Fuckin' right he is. (*Pause.*) You mean in the . . .
What d'you mean?

PADDY. In the faggot sense.

HUGHIE. *Ah*, no. I'm talkin' 'bout the insultin' sense, sense
he's one of the fucks makes . . .

PADDY. The cunts.

HUGHIE. . . . makes me bile sizzle. The cunts, I should say.
(*Beat.*)

PADDY. Should ring him back.

HUGHIE. I'm not goin' down the phone box that weather.

PADDY. You can wear me snorkel.

HUGHIE. I'm on'y goin' out if it's me oul'one. (*Pause.*)

PADDY. You know I called up, man?

HUGHIE. The hospital?

PADDY. Yeah. Family only, but.

HUGHIE. That's right. So you know it's serious. Every time
this thing goes off I think it's the hospital. They're the only
ones supposed to have me number in the *first* place. 'Course
Puppacat has to ask for it. An' not askin' but tellin'.

PADDY (*simultaneously with 'tellin''*). . . . Tellin'. Yeah.

HUGHIE. . . . Has to give it to Kilby then, so every time the
fuckin' thing beeps . . .

PADDY. Hums.

HUGHIE. . . . Whatever. Vib*rates* . . . I suspect the fuckin'
worst. You know?

PADDY. She's not *that* bad, is she? (*Pause.*) I mean, I know
she's *bad*, but I thought . . .

HUGHIE. You know what I'm sayin'? Me look, man?

PADDY. What?

HUGHIE. *Leave* it.

PADDY. Your look is sayin' leave it.

HUGHIE. I don't wanna talk about it. Although, thanks for callin' up an' all. 'Preciate it. As I'm sure she would've, mad as she is about you.

PADDY (*going over to trousers, turning them over*). An' me about her, man. Big time. So what did Bernie . . . ?

HUGHIE. Paddy.

PADDY. What?

HUGHIE. Your flute, man.

PADDY (*putting his flute back in*). Fuck sake! So what did Bernie Denk do you've to break his pins? No, first . . . *Did* he get up on his oul'one?

HUGHIE. You're obsessed with this.

PADDY. I wanna know what you heard.

HUGHIE. I heard, yeah. I heard maybe they had a, what would you . . . ? A relationship. A love affair. But there's no evidence, so . . .

PADDY. It's hearsay.

HUGHIE. Gossip. Yeah. It's inadmissible, so . . .

PADDY. Right. Go on.

HUGHIE. So, you know your woman reads the palms? Nancy.

PADDY. The cripple?

HUGHIE. She's not a cripple, man, she's minus a leg. She's a fuckin' . . .

PADDY. Peg.

HUGHIE. . . . Nancy with the peg-leg. Okay, well . . .

PADDY. I know her. She's a little tent down the West Yard.

HUGHIE. Right, well that's Puppacat's set up.

PADDY. Is it?!

HUGHIE. She goes up to his gaff, private consultations, star charts, the lot, right? He's into it an' 'parently she's accurate. Anyway. Last few weeks, seems Bernie Denk's hangin' 'round Nancy. Puppacat says he's been broachin' her in the street, accostin' her ominous. An' it's hard for her to 'scape the fuck . . .

PADDY. What with the . . .

HUGHIE. 'Zactly. How fast can you hoof it hoppin'? Hangin' round her tent an' all, but she doesn't wanna say an'thin' for the time *bein'*, 'cos . . .

PADDY. She hasn't gone to Puppacat?!

HUGHIE. This, no. This stage, he's just bein' a nuisance.

PADDY. What was he sayin' to her?

HUGHIE. The Puppa didn't say.

PADDY. An' why was he after her?

HUGHIE. Well, the Puppa didn't say, just . . .

PADDY. All right. Right . . . .

HUGHIE. So, *last* week, all right? Middle of the night, she hears noises out her back garden, she's in the sack, like, ganders out her window, who does she click only Bernie Denk. Bernie standin' there, ganderin' up . . .

PADDY. Scary stuff.

HUGHIE. Well. For a woman.

PADDY. That's what I mean.

HUGHIE. . . . Just ganderin' back at her. So she starts gettin' fretful. This is startin' to go *beyond* nuisance. Maybe he wants to commit rapeage or somethin'. *An'*, course, coupled with the *other* thing. Him gettin' up on his oul'one.

PADDY. The rumours.

HUGHIE. Y*eah*, the rumours. But if you're scared enough, rumours become fact, don't they? Bloke's out your back in the middle of the night, starin' up at your bedroom window, fuckin' . . . *madness* in his eyes . . . Far as you're gonna know or *want* to know, he's a pervert . . .

PADDY. The nightmare becomes reality.

HUGHIE. The nightmare, '*zactly* . . . Becomes, '*zactly*. An' it *did*, 'cos two nights later, the fucker breaks in, all right?

Breaks in, *wrecks* the place. He smashes a hole in her telly, tears the curtains to flits, the fridge, all the grub in her fridge, he fucks on the floor, tramples it. She's in the sack listenin' to all this an' what does she do . . . ?

PADDY. You're jokin'!

HUGHIE. . . . . Comes downstairs an' confronts him. What does *he* do but gives her a good hard kick in the peg-leg, kicks it so hard, he knocks it out from under her. She's standin' there, hoppin', should say, shoutin' at him, thinkin' righteous fuckin' indignation's gonna, you know . . .

PADDY. Women!

HUGHIE. . . . do the job . . .

PADDY. . . . Fucksake! *Bang!!!*

HUGHIE. Down she goes, whacks her knee off the ground. Smashes it. I says to Puppacat, Why've I to break *both* of Bernie's pins? Is one not enough? His reasonin's if *she* was incapacitated, which she is . . .

PADDY. She's *no* pins now.

HUGHIE. Well, she *has*, she's *one.*

PADDY. None that *work*, though.

HUGHIE. Then, no. Then he wants Bernie Denk put in the same situation an' may he be grateful we don't cut one of them *off* 'cos they don't grow back.

PADDY. They don't.

HUGHIE. It's gone, it's gone an' get used to fuckin' hoppin'. (*Pause.*)

PADDY. Would you get up on her?

HUGHIE. Nancy?

PADDY. Yeah.

HUGHIE. No, I wouldn't. But I wouldn't smash her knee either.

PADDY. Suppose, you do the deed, man, yeah?

HUGHIE. What's that?

PADDY. . . . You pay the fiddler. I don't see why *you* should be the one, but . . .

HUGHIE. 'Zactly.

PADDY. . . . has to . . .

HUGHIE. 'Zactly. *Be* the fuckin' fiddler. Just think they'd have a bit more sensitivity, the night that's in it.

PADDY. 'Zactly, man. Bit more tact an' all. (*Pause.*)

HUGHIE. D'you want another cuppa?

PADDY. Yeah.

HUGHIE (*picking up cups*). Think your trousers need a turnin'.

HUGHIE *exits.* PADDY *goes over to radiator, begins turning his trousers.* HUGHIE *re-enters, stands in the doorway.*

They dryin'?

PADDY. They're hot. (*Turning them.*) Don't know if they're dryin'.

HUGHIE. They're heatin', they're dryin'. (*Pause.*)

PADDY. What would you wear if you were me an' you were lookin' for a pair of trousers?

HUGHIE. Thought you weren't gettin' any.

PADDY. I'm just askin'.

HUGHIE. Well, d'you know what you like? (PADDY *thinks.*) All right, look . . . All right? I'm free Thursday . . .

PADDY. 'Head of you, man.

HUGHIE. . . . Poppin' Mossey's . . .

PADDY. An' I'm free too.

HUGHIE. A browsal . . . Good. . . . A perusal. You know, bit of a . . .

PADDY. 'Preciate it, man. An' I *do* know. Just, you know . . . I'm not lookin' for an entire wardrobe makeover.

HUGHIE. That's fine, Paddy. (*Exiting to kitchen.*) You're makin' a start, though.

PADDY (*to himself*). Just tryin' on some things, man.

> *Intercom buzzes.*

> Eh . . . Hughie?

> *Intercom buzzes.*

> Hughie!

> HUGHIE *enters, goes over to the intercom.*

HUGHIE (*into speaker*). Yeah?

KILBY'S VOICE. Don't 'Yeah' *me*, you cunt.

HUGHIE (*buzzing him in. To* PADDY). Kilby.

> HUGHIE *goes over to front door, opens it, puts it on the latch, heads back into kitchen. Pause. Enter* KILBY. *Short black leather jacket, umbrella, blond perm.*

KILBY. Hughie? (*To* PADDY.) Where is he? (*Calling.*) Hughie! (*To* PADDY.) Fuckin' hack of this place!

> HUGHIE *enters with two cups of tea, stops in the doorway.*

> (*To* HUGHIE.) The fuck are you doin'? (*To* PADDY.) Story, fuckhead?

PADDY. What's the jack?

KILBY. Give that a shakin', will you? (*Hands umbrella to* PADDY. *To* HUGHIE.) The fuck're you doin'?

HUGHIE (*putting tea on table*). What?

KILBY. I'm after comin' all the way down here in a blazin' fuckin' . . . in a monsoon, man. Hadn't got me brolly, I'd be fuckin' *drenched*, I would. (*To* PADDY.) That right Paddy? *Shake* the fuckin' thing. Drowned, I'd'a been. (*Looks at* PADDY'*s boxers*.) The fuck were youse faggots up to? (*To* HUGHIE.) What am I after walkin' in on? Is this a fuckin' . . . Is this one of them rendez-vous or somethin'?

PADDY. Me pants are wet.

KILBY. Your fuckin' *pants?!!*

HUGHIE. His trousers.

KILBY. I . . . (*To* HUGHIE.) Right. (*Beat. To* PADDY.) They're wet?!

PADDY. The *rain*, man.

KILBY. Oh. Had you no brolly? Will you *shake* the fuckin'
thing? I thought youse were suckin' each other's cocks or
somethin'. (*To* HUGHIE.) Here, fuckhead. The fuck's
wrong with you, you can't answer your beeper, huh? Have
me out there bravin' the hurricane.

HUGHIE. Was waitin' 'till it relented, man.

KILBY. Have you no sense of manhood about yourself a'tall,
no? No sense of the machiz, you couldn't go 'round the
corner? It's only a shower, the name of fuck. (*To* PADDY.)
Should be dry, man.

PADDY *continues to shake umbrella.*

Paddy?

PADDY *stops.*

Should be dry.

PADDY *leans umbrella against wall, sits back down.*

(*To* HUGHIE.) It's only a fuckin' drizzle. D'you know what
I mean? Tell him, Paddy.

PADDY. Ah, well . . . Have to disagree now, Kilby. I've been
there, you know? Experienced a bit more than a drizzle.

KILBY. What did you experience?

PADDY. *I* don't know, but . . .

KILBY. *Well*, then. (*Short pause. To* HUGHIE.) Hughie . . .

PADDY. . . . A Deluge or somethin'.

KILBY (*pause*). You wouldn't know a deluge if it hit you on
the fuckin' head, you prick. (*To* HUGHIE.) An' that's why
you didn't answer?! That's bad. (*To* PADDY.) You smart
prick, you, Paddy. (*To* HUGHIE.) That's bad, now. If that
winchy measure of respect's all Kilby commands, then
maybe he'll have to . . . (*Mimes the action of taking a badge
from his chest and throwing it down.*) throw down the tin
badge, give up his deputyhood, you know what I'm sayin',
Paddy? Step outside the law prevents the dispensin' of swift
justice. (*Miming.*) Just below the ribcage. Fuckin' rupture
you. Would you like that? Don't think you would. (*Short
pause. To* HUGHIE.) Would *you?*

HUGHIE. No.

KILBY. Didn't think you would. Think you'd like gettin' wet better, wouldn't you? Think you'd face the deluge as your man says, quicker than a . . . (*Miming.*) phoenix eye fist below the ribcage from Kilby. All right, Paddy? What's your cock doin' on your lap?

PADDY (*looking down*). Fuckin' . . . Agh !! (*Puts his cock away.*)

KILBY. You notice *he* wouldn't tell you? Could've been restin' there all night, he wouldn't open his mouth. But you'd notice his *eyes* lingerin' all right. Be lickin' his chops, he would. (*To* HUGHIE.) Wouldn't you, man?

HUGHIE. I would.

KILBY. I *know* you would. Don't need to fuckin' tell me. (*To* PADDY.) Moistenin' his lips, he'd be, an' fidgetin'. Adjustin' his crotch an' all.

HUGHIE. D'you wanna cuppa, Kilby?

KILBY. Fuck that tea shit.

HUGHIE. Coffee?

KILBY. Maybe it's fuckin' coffee I want. Are you not supposed to be pin breakin'?

HUGHIE. I am.

KILBY. You can no more pin break than I can fuckin' . . . stroke me twat, man. When are you doin' it?

HUGHIE. In a while.

KILBY. Don't give me this obscure shit, man.

HUGHIE. 'Bout an hour.

KILBY. . . . Don't Mister Miyagi me. An hour?! You've to do it sooner.

HUGHIE. Well, I'll . . .

KILBY. No. No. You've to do it sooner. He's at home, now. What happens you call up, he's gone out?

HUGHIE. I don't know.

KILBY. . . . Huh?

HUGHIE. I do it tomorrow?

KILBY. But Puppacat's payin' you to do it today. May not pay you a'tall, may get rancorous instead, man, have to *be* a puppy, you know? Send Kilby down to . . . (*Miming.*) break your kneecap with a footstomp. Now, I'm after ringin' the cunt, all right? That's one of the 'vantages of havin' a phone.

HUGHIE. Kilby, you're the one wrecked it.

KILBY. Axe-kick, Paddy.

PADDY. Yeah?

KILBY. Booze an' karate, man. (*To* HUGHIE.) Rang the cunt, he's in, Hughie. (*To* PADDY.) Destructive combo. (*To* HUGHIE.) He's in, he's the prime of health. Get up there an' break his pins 'fore he splits out an' you can't. Okay?

HUGHIE. Right. I'll just . . .

KILBY. Just finish your tea, get your fuckin' arse up there. (*Picks up* PADDY*'s video cassette.*) This yours, Paddy?

PADDY. Yeah.

KILBY. This the one with the bit . . . .? Which *is* it?

PADDY. Which?

KILBY. Fights the fat fucker?

PADDY. Yeah.

KILBY. . . . . Batters him. Some good fuckin' bits in that. Youse watchin' it after?

PADDY. Yeah.

KILBY. Wouldn't mind seein' that, now. Could I watch it with youse?

HUGHIE. I've to do this, Kilby.

KILBY. How long d'you think it takes? You're not fixin' the fuck, you're breakin' him. Paddy'll still be here when you get back. (*To* PADDY.) Won't you? (*To* HUGHIE.) With his cock hangin' out all steamy. So go, come back, we'll watch Bruce do it proper. Yeah? Watch him break *more* than pins. (*To* PADDY.) Bit in this where he breaks your man's neck?

PADDY. Whose?

KILBY. Some fuck's.

PADDY. He breaks a couple.

KILBY. Yeah?

PADDY. Breaks a few.

KILBY. Lookin' forward, then. (*To* HUGHIE.) Oh, how's the oul'one, man? Jaysus, I nearly forgot. (*To* PADDY.) Fuckin' oul'one in hospital. (*To* HUGHIE.) C'mere. Puppacat says to tell you he's sorry for askin' you to do this while . . . You know, felt a bit bad about it. (*To* PADDY.) Complimented me there on me perm, she did.

PADDY. Yeah?

KILBY. Thought it was fuckin' dapper. How *is* she?

HUGHIE. I'd rather not talk about it, man. (*Short pause.*) 'F you don't mind, like.

KILBY. You'd rather not talk about it?! Jays, don't talk to Kilby, who the fuck can you talk to?

HUGHIE. 'Preciate that, man. You know?

KILBY. Ah, sure . . .

HUGHIE. Do. 'Preciate your interest. '*But* . . . ' (*Beat.*) You know . . . ? Have to say, now, '*But* . . . '

KILBY (*to* PADDY). Bit offensive that, whatsay, Paddy? Lack of confidence in Kilby?

HUGHIE. It's not, man, it's just that . . .

KILBY. Lack of trust an' all? Find it a bit hard to reconcile meself to that now, Hughie. But, all right, man. Fuck it. You don't wanna tell me, don't. (*Beat.*) '*But* . . . '

HUGHIE. Well . . .

KILBY. '*But* . . . ' (*Beat.*) You know what I'm sayin'?

HUGHIE (*pause*). She's still in intensive care, all right? She's there, she's stable, they're monitorin' her, like, she hasn't gotten any worse, but . . .

PADDY. Still an' all.

KILBY. Right. Still . . . .

HUGHIE. . . . It's fuckin' intensive care.

KILBY (*pause*). Empathy, man. You know? Seriously. Sympathy. (*To* PADDY.) She never cusses.

PADDY. That's right.

KILBY (*to* HUGHIE). Does she?

HUGHIE. No.

KILBY (*to* PADDY). Never fuckin' cusses. (*Long pause.*) So she's in there, safe, anyway, bit of tender lovin' . . . ?

HUGHIE. Yeah.

KILBY. She'll be all right. Don't worry about it for fuck's sake. (*To* PADDY.) Paddy?

PADDY. She will, she'll be fine.

KILBY. An' what about this dirtbird?

HUGHIE. Which?

KILBY. Dirtbird crashed her.

HUGHIE. What *about* him?

KILBY. I don't know. (*Beat.*) . . . You know? You tell *me*.

HUGHIE. Tell you what?

KILBY. *I'm* askin' *you*, man. (*Pause. To* PADDY.) D'you get me, Paddy?

PADDY. What?

KILBY. You not spottin' where I'm headin'?

PADDY. Well, I'm *tailin'* you. But, eh . . .

KILBY. You don't know where I'm bound.

PADDY. . . . Didn't spot that, no.

KILBY. Payback, man.

PADDY *coughs.*

Gallopin' consumption. (*To* HUGHIE.) Taste of the lash, whatsay, Hughie?

PADDY *coughs.*

That's gallopin' consumption, man. (*To* HUGHIE.) Grind the fucker up like he ground . . . (*Short pause.*) em . . .

PADDY. Dolly.

KILBY. I know her name, man. (*To* HUGHIE.) Whatsay?
Cook him in a pot. Mangle the cunt like he mangled Dolly.
(*To* PADDY.) See? No need to tell me. (*To* HUGHIE.) Like
he mangled your *oul'* one.

HUGHIE. Listen. Kilby . . .

KILBY. Your mother.

HUGHIE. . . . Grateful's I *am*, man. Your interest, concern, all
that. Empathy . . .

KILBY. Sympathy.

HUGHIE. All that . . . Thankful's I *am* . . . (*Short pause.*) I've
no interest at the moment. No offence. She's still in the
critical, you know? I've more on me mind than . . .

KILBY. All right . . .

HUGHIE. . . . than fuckin' . . .

KILBY. . . . right. No need to reproof me, man. Jaysus. Just
tryin' to offer me help. (*To* PADDY.) D'you hear him
reproofin' me?

HUGHIE. I'm not reproofin'. She's old, she's broken to bits. I
haven't a clue what parts'll be workin', she gets out, what
parts won't, if she *makes* it out 'cos there's a big chance she
won't. Find it hard to separate me mind, you see, me
emotions from what's goin' on with her, d'you understand
me? Sure, I'm not too gleeful 'bout doin' *this* thing.

KILBY. What?

HUGHIE. This Denk shit. I've more on me mind the night
that's fuckin' *in* it.

KILBY (*pause*). Well, d'you want *me* to go up an' do it?

HUGHIE. Right.

KILBY. No. Hughie . . .

HUGHIE. What?

KILBY. *Do* you?

Long pause. PADDY *coughs.*

(*To* PADDY.) Cancer, man.

PADDY (*coughs again*). Fucksake!

KILBY. Tuberculosis, that is. (*To* HUGHIE.) Get up there, Hughie . . .

PADDY. Fuckin' *flu*, I think.

KILBY. . . . All right? Break Bernie's pins an' make Puppacat proud. An' the Kilby. (*Winks*.) Goes without sayin'.

HUGHIE *finishes his tea, goes to* PADDY, *stands over him*.

PADDY. What?

HUGHIE. You finished?

PADDY *gives him cup and he exits. Silence.* KILBY *picks up tape again.*

KILBY. What's this 'Eight Diagram Pole Fighters' about?

PADDY. 'Bout these eh . . .

KILBY. Pole fighters?

PADDY. Yeah.

KILBY. They baldy?

PADDY. They are, yeah. Monks.

KILBY. Think I seen it.

Silence. HUGHIE *enters with baseball bat, goes over to window, looks out.*

HUGHIE. Lend us your brolly, Kilby.

KILBY. Sorry, man. Might wanna go out, get treats or somethin'. Goodies.

PADDY. You can borry me snorkel if you want.

Pause. HUGHIE *gives him a look.*

Ah, fuck you!

HUGHIE (*grabbing one of his own jackets, putting it on angrily*). Fuckin' snorkel! I'd rather get up on Obboe the fuckin' Abbo . . . You know Obboe?

KILBY. Ooh . . . !

HUGHIE. . . . On O'Connell Street or somethin'.

KILBY. . . . Fuck! In public?

HUGHIE *exits, slamming door.*

Nasty, man. (*Pause.*) Cheek of the fuck, huh?

PADDY. Fuckin' Obboe the Abbo!

KILBY. Don't mind him, man. (*Goes over to the window.*) Cheeky cunt *like* him. (*Looks down at the street.*) There he goes, look? The fuckin' eejit. (*Pause.*) Paddy.

PADDY *joins him.*

Drowned, he'll be. Any grub here?

PADDY. Dunno.

KILBY. Bit of hunger, I have.

KILBY *exits to kitchen.* PADDY *looks out the window once more.*

(*Off.*) Ever have nik-nax, man?

PADDY (*returning to his chair*). Which're they?

KILBY (*off*). Crip things. You suck them. (*Enters.*) Suck all the flavour out, then chew.

PADDY. No.

KILBY. Taste of spare ribs. You like crips?

PADDY. *Some* crips.

KILBY. Right. You'd think he'd have somethin' gourmet in stock all the same; some veg or the like. (*Sits down.*)

PADDY. Whatever happened that chink writin' jacket you used to have, Kilby?

KILBY. Dragon Fist.

PADDY. That what it said?

KILBY. It's a northern system. Shaolin.

PADDY. Kinda had a feelin' it said somethin' Karate, now.

KILBY. Fuckin' thing was stroked on me. You know . . . ? Nah, you wouldn't.

PADDY. Who?

KILBY. . . . CopperDolan.

PADDY. I *do* know him.

KILBY. Stroked it off me thirty year back.

PADDY (*going over to snorkel*). See this?

KILBY. How *d'you* know him?

PADDY (*of rip*). See that?

KILBY. . . . Paddy!

PADDY. I'm tellin' you, man. See how it's ripped, it's wrecked?

KILBY. Yeah.

PADDY. CopperDolan fucked me in a puddle tonight. Beset me me way over.

KILBY. The fat fuck! He *beset* you?!

PADDY. Hughie reckons it's 'cos I was seen with him . . .

KILBY (*simultaneous with 'seen with him'*). . . . Seen with him. Probly right. Probly thought you were an echelon. Hates Puppacat . . .

PADDY. Yeah?

KILBY. . . . Hates, *Oh*, yeah. Hates us all, the fuckin' menace! But with the agreement an' all, the treaty . . .

PADDY. An' he stroked it on you.

KILBY. You know Delgado's over the gook nation? Down there one night, coupla games. Took a shine to it, he did, liked the cut. Stuck it on his back an' sauntered out the door, guffawin' . . .

PADDY *does Dolan's laugh*.

Fuck could I do? Not bad, man.

PADDY. Cheers.

KILBY. Not *great*, now. But, fuck could I do?

PADDY. He's a copper.

KILBY. That's it, an' he's mad.

PADDY. The fuck d'you do?

KILBY. Keep your mouth shut an' your eye on the black 'cos it's bait. You get me?

PADDY. He wanted to rile you.

KILBY. To bait me for a batterin'. Same reason he beset yourself, man. (*Pause.*)

PADDY. Used to think that jacket was great, you know that . . . ?

KILBY. It *was* great.

PADDY. . . . See you walkin' down the street, think, Jaysus! I wish I had a fuckin' chink writin' jacket.

KILBY. That jacket was a one of a kind, man. Hand*made*, hand*stitched* . . .

PADDY. Who stitched it?

KILBY. Who d'you think?

PADDY. Well *done*, man.

KILBY. Bit of craftsmanship for you. (*Indicating his own jacket.*) That one there's the same make, now, same leather an' all, but it's *not* the same, you know? I'd me Dragon Fist yonks.

PADDY. Same here.

KILBY. Your snorkel?

PADDY. Donkeys, man.

KILBY. See, Hughie knows nothin'. He's gonna come back pissed on, now. An' why? 'Cos he wouldn't . . . wear . . . the functional . . . item. Got the values of a woman, he has. Woman'd walk six miles nippy through a blizzard, you know? Give herself frostbite on the buds to show off a ring in her pissflap. He's the same. Stop buyin' jacks roll if muck was in fashion, do his day to day, dirty brown between his legs. Fuckin' designer shirt . . .

PADDY. John Rocha.

KILBY. That a Rocha?

PADDY. So he said.

KILBY. Fuck sake. See, this is what I'm talkin' 'bout. I mean, you ask me 'bout clothes, I'll tell you . . . You know, if you *ask* me. Say about . . . (*Pause.*) What?

PADDY. I dunno, jackets?

KILBY. You askin' me?!

PADDY. Yeah.

KILBY. Same as yourself, man, same as meself. Snorkel, a
good leather . . . You *know* jackets. What else?

PADDY. Pants? Trousers?

KILBY. 'Bout trousers, I'll tell you. Combats. All right? Combats. Strong. Baggy. Style an' function. Now. Baggies . . .
Right? Why baggies?

PADDY (*short pause*). They're baggy?

KILBY. 'Zactly. Function. Room. Movement. Jeans, now.
Jeans, the same thing.

PADDY. I . . . Well . . .

KILBY. What?

PADDY. . . . I wouldn't've thought . . .

KILBY. 'Cos they're tight? Constrictive? That what you're
sayin'? (*Hand on crotch.*) 'Cos they bind your packet?

PADDY. Yeah.

KILBY. Not Action Jeans, man.

PADDY. What?!

KILBY. Not Chuck Norris Action Jeans. Chucks've a hidden
gusset in the packet area so's you can get your leg up high,
get that kick action goin', you know? (*Bends over.*) See it?
Little gusset in there under me bollox?

PADDY. Oh, yeah.

KILBY. Chuck wears them on his ranch. I mean I couldn't do
a high roundhouse in a normal pair, for instance, spinnin'
hook kick . . .

PADDY. Right.

KILBY. . . . No gusset, man. Can't get the leg up. But with the
Chuck jeans . . . Think about it. Function. Room.
Movement. (*Modelling.*) An' they *look* good as well. So it's
style in harmony with em . . .

PADDY. Practicality.

KILBY. That's it.

PADDY. Well, that's what I'd be interested in.

KILBY. I've order forms at home. Have to send away the States. D'you wanna couple?

PADDY. Yeah.

KILBY. See what I can do, man. Jaysus, the oul' belly's gettin' a bit leppin'. Might have them nik-nax, calm it down. (*Short pause.*) Ungourmet's they are.

PADDY *coughs.*

Whoopin' cough, is it?

PADDY. Fuckin' *flu*, man.

KILBY. 'Flu!' Spoonful of Venos's all that needs. (*Short pause.*) Bit of a hoopman, Paddy, aren't you.

PADDY. I am in me hole a hoopman.

KILBY. No wonder Hughie's reluctant to do the business, the likes of you gayin' him up. Hate to see you get a dig, now, you'd fall down, probly *stay* down.

PADDY. I'd get up.

KILBY. Would you, now?

PADDY. Get up an' walk tall, I would. Hit back hard.

KILBY. A big man? Not CopperDolan, like, but someone else big?

PADDY. If he hit me.

KILBY. . . . Like Bernie Denk, say. Reckon you could lick a heifer like Bernie ? Huh ? Break his pins for a penny or two? (*Pause.*) I'm not askin' you to *do* it, man. I'm just askin' if you think you've the fibre, the sand for that kinda fuckin' *activity.*

PADDY (*pause*). I reckon so.

KILBY. Reckon so too, man.

PADDY. Do you ?

KILBY. Well, let's say I've reason to believe. Have that hunch about you, I do. So, d'you know any moves ?

PADDY. Headbutts an' shit ?

KILBY. Fuck headbutts. Techniques, man. Karate, fucksake, put your man down, disempower the cunt.

PADDY. Not really.

KILBY. You should. That's somethin' Hughie never learnt, he'll regret. Coupla lessons with Kilby if you want, set you straight. (*Short pause.*) Fuck this, man.

> KILBY *exits, pause. Enters with nik-nax, stands at doorway, opens packet, puts one in his mouth, sucks.*

PADDY. You actually know the arts, Kilby? (*Pause.*) Kilby. (*Pause.* KILBY *still sucking.*) Kilby, man.

KILBY (*starts chewing*). Fuck d'you think I know the lingo, man? *Or* the moves. Can't know the lingo an' the moves without knowin' the fuckin' art. (*Puts another one in his mouth, sucks.*)

PADDY. An' what like . . . belt would you . . . ?

> KILBY *shakes his head. Pause. Sucks five or six seconds, chews.*

KILBY. Black. Second dan. Goin' for me third. D'you want one? (*Short pause.*) Go on. Taste of spare ribs.

PADDY. What do I do?

KILBY. Suck them.

> PADDY *takes one, puts it in his mouth and sucks.* KILBY *likewise. Pause, seven or eight seconds. They chew,* PADDY *nodding.*

Get all the flavour?

PADDY. Jaysus.

KILBY. Savoury, aren't they?

PADDY. Salty.

KILBY. Yeah . . . That's what savoury fuckin' *means*, man. (*Short pause.*) Think I feel somthin' brown brewin', now. (*Short pause.*) Shotokan.

PADDY. Huh?

KILBY. That's me school, man. Me discipline. Thirty percent fists, seventy legs. Hence the fuckin' . . . me Chuck jeans. Me gusset. Weapon of choice is the pole.

PADDY (*of nik-nax*). Delicious.

KILBY. You listenin'?! An' not *this* fuckin' pole. (*Grabs crotch.*) A longer pole for fightin'. But not *much* longer, think you know what I'm sayin'. (*Winks.*)

PADDY. An' can you smash bricks an' shit?

KILBY (*holds out his hands*). See them calluses? (PADDY *looks.*) Make no mistake, man. (*Of nik-nax.*) Might have some of them after for durin' the film, huh? Might send you out. (*Pause, sucking his fingers.*) Time you.

PADDY. Give us another one.

KILBY. One more. (*Giving him one.*) Make the most of it.

They suck seven or eight seconds before chewing.

Don't know will I go up yet.

PADDY. Where?

KILBY (*lifts his buttocks slightly off chair. Pause*). It's approachin' the lips of me hoop. (*Pause. Considering, then sitting back down.*) Fuck it. What d'you think of this place?

PADDY. Nice.

KILBY. I think it's a hole.

PADDY. You know what you are, Kilby? Have to say . . .

KILBY. What's that?

PADDY. You're the deputy sheriff of fuckin' . . . of crip.

KILBY. You clever cunt.

PADDY. Aren't you?

KILBY. That's *exactly* what I am. (*Short pause.*) Of crip an' of batterin'. (*Takes another from the packet, holds it in front of his mouth.*) Sorry man. Rest are for Kilby. (*Puts it in his mouth, sucks five or six seconds, scrunching the bag closed, then, chewing.*) That's really pissed me off now, you know that ? 'Bout your snorkel an' all. Kind of ingrained on me brain.

PADDY. Ah, he's always at that.

KILBY. . . . Branded in there. I know he's under pressure, but there's ways to talk to your mates. (*Pause. To himself.*) 'The deputy sheriff of crips'.

PADDY. Crip.

KILBY. ' . . . Of crip'. Even better. (*Pause.*) Class fuckin' phrase, that. (*To* PADDY.) 'Cos I *like* crips, I do. (*Pause.*) *Like* savoury. (*Pause. Fidgets a little on chair.*) That's it, now. (*Beat.*) Is it? (*Half stands up.*) Yep. It's touchin' cloth. (*Stands up, exiting.*) Gonna flush me quarry, man.

> KILBY *exits.* PADDY *goes over to his trousers and turns them. Goes over to* KILBY*'s jacket, feels it, admires it. Takes jacket off coat-rack. The toilet flushes. Quickly puts jacket back on coat rack. Jacket falls on floor. Picks it up again and hangs it up just as* KILBY *enters.*

Fuck're you doin'?

PADDY. Just admirin'.

KILBY. Go easy! (*Sits down.*)

PADDY (*running his hand along back of jacket*). Was downwards, wasn't it.

KILBY. That's the way chink *goes,* man. Downwards or backwards.

PADDY. Dragon Fist.

KILBY. Northern Shaolin school. Now get away from it.

PADDY (*sits down*). An' it was pre*cisely* fuckin' stitched, wasn't it?

KILBY. Took a month an' a half.

PADDY. Jaysus! (*Pause.*) An' would you not ask Puppacat to get a few echelons together, like, yourself, Hughie an' all an' just, you know, *do* somethin'.

KILBY. 'Bout CopperDolan?

PADDY. *To* him.

KILBY. He's a copper, Paddy. There's rules, man, the treaty. We can't fuck with him.

PADDY. But he can fuck with us.

KILBY. Outs . . .

PADDY. *Youse.*

KILBY. Outside the boundaries he can do what he wants. An'
I know Puppacat's talked to him 'bout goin' easy in general,
but yeah, he's still there, man. Causin' hassle, fuckin' . . .

PADDY. Like Serpico.

KILBY. Who?

PADDY. The film.

KILBY (*pause*). Karate film?

PADDY. Pacino, man. Coppers.

KILBY. Didn't see it. An' why's he like him?

PADDY. Bit of a righteous cunt.

KILBY. CopperDolan's not righteous.

PADDY. Well, I know, but . . .

KILBY. Sure how could he be, cahootin' with wicked cunts
like us, makin' villainous treaties an' all? CopperDolan's a
half-rogue fuckin' maverick, spends half his beat down
Delgados playin' pool an' gettin' his billy-club sucked gratis
by hooers.

PADDY. He's into that, yeah?

KILBY. Which?

PADDY. That kind of act.

KILBY. *Oh,* yeah. Pig in shite, man. See, the gook nation's his
beat so no one keeps an eye on him. Get them to come in,
he will, one or two a night. He'll have a couple of games,
few pints an' a hooverin'. An' *dogs,* man . . .

PADDY. Yeah?

KILBY. . . . *Jaysus! But* . . . You know? Long's they're a mouth
an' a tongue an' some power of good suction . . .

PADDY. . . . He's a happy copper.

KILBY. 'Zactly. (*Pause.*) Like to give him a spankin', I would.

PADDY. Like to meself.

KILBY. Good buggerin'.

PADDY. What?

KILBY. An' not in a sexual way, now. Not in a way he'd like it, pansy an' all's he is, but in a violent way. Disable him with a wing-chun flurry, stun the cunt, I would, then stick it up there, snap his hoop for him, bugger him with a tearin' forceful motion. Powerful motion he wouldn't like. Bugger resistance out of him. Then I'd sit him down with a needle an' thread, make him sew Dragon Fist onto *that* jacket.

PADDY. Good idea.

KILBY. Have me lob out like this, I would. He'd be bent over bareholed, beaverin' away an' every time he made a mistake, I'd – Uuh! – slide it up a bit, there, just an inch or two, maybe three. As a threat, you know ?

PADDY. Of the *full* bugger, yeah?

KILBY. Full length an' hornspread, man. As a taster. Unh! An' I'd be sayin' . . . Give his arse a little spank, there, too, (*Mimes a slap on Dolan's arse with sound effect.*) bit of a shamin' spank an' I'd be sayin' . . . The fuck'd I be sayin'?

PADDY (*pause*). You want *me* to . . . ?

KILBY (*simultaneous with 'to'*). I'm askin' you, fuck sake.

PADDY. I don't know. Em . . .

KILBY. No?

PADDY. Em . . .

KILBY. '*Get* that fuckin' thing done.'

PADDY. Right.

KILBY. 'Now!'

PADDY. 'An' no mistakes'.

KILBY. 'Or it'll be the full hog an' rimstrain'.

PADDY. Rimstrain. *Ring*sprain.

KILBY. . . . Fuckin, *yeah.* Unh! 'You feel it, CopperDolan?' Unh! 'You feel the potential, there, man?'

PADDY. Potential for anguish.

KILBY. 'You feel it? (*Mimes arseslap.*) Huh? Gonna stop you destroyin'. Treaty or not, man. Treaty or none, gonna make you create.'

PADDY. 'Or suffer'.

KILBY. Yep.

PADDY. 'Create or suffer, man. Create or endure. *Your* choice'.

KILBY. 'Vicious full length buggerin' or, or . . . '

PADDY. ' . . . Sewin''.

KILBY. '*Sewin'!*' Fuckin' *needle*craft, man.

PADDY. 'Buggerin' or needlecraft, CopperDolan'.

KILBY. 'One or the other'.

PADDY (*self-consciously*). Unh!

KILBY. Unh! *Oh,* yeah.

PADDY. 'That hurt, CopperDolan?'

KILBY. 'That hurt, man?'

PADDY/KILBY (*simultaneously*). 'Well, it's meant to'. (*Slight laugh.*)

KILBY. 'Cos playin' with Kilby, you're playin' with fire . . . '

PADDY. Uh-huh . . .

KILBY. Like it?

PADDY. I do.

KILBY. What else?

PADDY. ' . . . So you're gonna get burnt'

KILBY. Nah, that's a continuation.

PADDY. It is. Of . . .

KILBY. Go on.

PADDY. . . . Of the other . . .

KILBY. Go on. Somethin' else.

PADDY. Em. 'You were nasty, man.' Yeah?

KILBY. Unh! *Yeah,* man. Nasty to Kilby. (*Mimes arseslap.*)
'To his jacket.'

PADDY. 'So now Kilby's gonna be nasty'. (*Mimes arseslap.*)

KILBY. Unh!

PADDY. Yeah?

KILBY. Go on, man.

PADDY. . . . Nasty to the CopperDolan'. (*Mimes arseslap.*)
Unh!

KILBY. Unh! (*Mimes arseslap.*)

PADDY (*mimes arseslap*).

KILBY (*mimes arseslap*). Unh!

PADDY. Unh!

KILBY. Fuckin' Unh, man!!! You've more style in your . . .
(*Mimes arseslap.*) in your little fuckin' *finger!*

PADDY. Thanks.

KILBY. . . . In your *flute* than Hughie has!

PADDY. Give us another one of them nik-nax, will you?

KILBY. Sorry, man. Nik-nax stay with Kilby. See, Hughie's
clothes have style, you can't dispute that, polly an' all's it is,
but the man *inside* the clothes . . . ? Sorely lackin' I reckon.
An' I'm not puttin' him down, now, I know he's your mate,
what I'm doin's questionin'. I mean, who am I to say
straight out he's an arse or a fuckhead or, I don't know, a
shitpoke, when he's got, you know, people like yourself
really like him, Puppacat an' all . . . ?

PADDY. Puppacat?

KILBY. *Weell*, he's *fond* of him. But what I'm sayin's just 'cos
he thinks one thing, doesn't mean I can't observe an'
question, me own self, does it?

PADDY. 'Course not.

KILBY. . . . Follow me *own* hunches. That's me way, man.
(*Standing up.*) C'mon. Show you a few moves.

PADDY. What?

KILBY. You said you wanted a lesson. Let's go. Get up there an' take the stance.

PADDY *stands up.*

All this mimin' of buttfuck has me riled up. (*Takes out nik-nax.*) Here. (*Gives one to* PADDY.) Fortify us for the session.

KILBY *takes one himself and they suck, six to eight seconds, then chew.*

PADDY. Hang on a sec', man. Sorry . . . Just to go back . . .

KILBY (*doing stretching exercises*). What?!

PADDY. You said about the Puppacat bein' fond of Hughie an' all?!

KILBY. Mmm-Hmm.

PADDY. Yeah?

KILBY. *Yeah,* man.

PADDY. Well if he feels that way, then why's he makin' him go up an' break Bernie Denk's pins when he knows he's all fucked up over his oul' one?

KILBY. *Ah* . . .

PADDY. . . . You know?

KILBY (*stops stretching*). . . . Well . . . Maybe he doesn't *have* to. Maybe all's not what it seems an' Hughie's gonna get a surprise when he gets up to Bernie's. Puppacat works in wondrous ways, man. Don't underestimate his power to go all corkscrewy, lep off the beaten track, know what I'm sayin'? Go the less travelled.

PADDY. What's the surprise?

KILBY. Surprise, man.

PADDY. Huh?

KILBY. It's a surprise. (*Heading towards toilet.*) Goin' for a shite. Get ready.

PADDY. Again?!

KILBY. Once you break the seal, man. An' shut the fuck up! You countin'?

PADDY. No.

KILBY. Had *half,* man.

> KILBY *exits.* PADDY *goes over to his jacket, puts it on, gets a feel for it. He tries a karate kick, admires himself, tries a different kick. His cock falls out of his boxers. He puts it back in. The toilet flushes. He takes the jacket off quickly, hangs it up, sits down.* KILBY *enters.*

> Right. Take the stance.

PADDY. Ah, you're all right, Kilby.

KILBY. What . . . ?

PADDY. You're grand.

KILBY. Did I *say* there was somethin' wrong with me, Paddy?

PADDY. No.

KILBY. Then shut the fuck up . . . *get* up . . . an' take the fuckin' stance.

PADDY (*pause*). Can you not just *tell* me?

KILBY. Can you *tell* someone how to swim, Paddy? No. You've to fuck them in the water. So . . . Actually, hang on. You mind puttin' your trousers on first? Don't want your flute fallin' out when we're in close contact. D'you mind?

> PADDY *gets his trousers off the radiator and begins putting them on.*

> Dirty, wriggly thing. Don't get me wrong, man. I'm sure certain birds like it, possibly Hughie, whatever. Just that compared to me *own* . . . in me own *opinion,* like . . . it's a bit fuckin' wriggly. (*Short pause.*) D'you take that personal?

PADDY. No.

KILBY. Good. Take the stance.

> *The door opens and* HUGHIE *enters, soaking wet. He walks by without even looking at them.*

KILBY. Well . . . ?

HUGHIE. Very clever, aren't you?

> HUGHIE *exits left. Pause.*

PADDY. What's he on about ?

KILBY. None of your business. C'mon an' I'll show you the one 'fore he comes back in.

PADDY. Aah, now . . .

KILBY. . . . C'mon. Show you a lock, I will. An arm lock you can do with one hand an' keep the other one free to inflict damage, pull your lob or whatever. (*Beat*.) All right?

PADDY. Why's he sayin' you're clever?

KILBY. 'Cos I *am,* man. Now, c'mere an' try an' grab me.

Pause. PADDY *goes to grab him.*

Wait. No. Wait. Try an' hit me a dig.

PADDY. Hit you a . . . ?

KILBY. That's right. Try an' hit me a wallop. (*Pause*.) I won't hurt you, Paddy.

PADDY. You swear?

KILBY. Don't doubt me precision, man, me control. All right? Have faith in me skill as your sensei. Now go.

Pause. KILBY *takes a defensive stance.* PADDY *gets ready to attack.* HUGHIE *enters, interrupting them. He wears dry trousers and a t-shirt, carries a towel.*

KILBY. Did you wreck your Rocha, man?

PADDY. Should've wore me snorkel, Hughie.

HUGHIE sits down in an armchair.

The offer was there.

HUGHIE begins drying his hair.

KILBY (*to* PADDY). Do it after, yeah?

PADDY. Which ? Oh, right.

KILBY. The *moves,* man.

HUGHIE finishes drying his hair. Silence.

KILBY. Well . . . ? (*Pause*.) Hughie.

HUGHIE. What?

KILBY. Tell.

HUGHIE. Nothin' *to* tell, man. Who left stink?

KILBY. Stink?

HUGHIE. In me jacks.

KILBY (*pause*). I think if you go back in, Hughie, take a good sniff, you'll discover you're mistaken there. It's not a stink, it's a hum.

HUGHIE. A hum?

KILBY. A sweet, healthy hum. My stools don't stink. Now tell us about up Bernie's.

HUGHIE (*pause. To* PADDY). D'*you* know about this?

PADDY. What?

HUGHIE. . . . No?

KILBY. 'Bout what, Hughie?

HUGHIE. You *know* what. The bloke up Bernie's. The fuckin' driver.

KILBY. *Aaaah,* right. Driver in the chair . . .

PADDY. Who's this?

KILBY. . . . Tied up.

HUGHIE. Tied up in the chair, minus *teeth*, you cunt. Fuckin' Bernie Denk in leather fuckin' gloves, isn't that it.

KILBY. Work gloves.

HUGHIE. Me thinkin' *he's* the one whose pins I'm s'pposed to be breakin' an' there he is, workin' your man over, leather gloves an' brass knucks, smackin' him 'round, he's after knockin' half his teeth out. An' *that* mad cunt, that peg legged cunt, hoppin' round.

PADDY. Who's it, Nancy?

HUGHIE. Nancy *an'* Bernie.

KILBY. The lovers.

PADDY. Huh?

KILBY (*to* PADDY). *Oh,* yeah.

HUGHIE. . . . Hoppin' round behind me like a pogo stick, hasn't the common fuckin' manners to wear her prosthetic. Up an' down, up an' down, over me shoulder, talkin' in me fuckin' ear, 'I predict this, I predict that . . . '

KILBY. What'd she predict ?

HUGHIE. A batterin'. Fuck d'you think ?

KILBY. Receivin' or givin' ?

HUGHIE. You *know,* givin'. Predictin' me gettin' in there, Paddy, givin' your man one 's if he wasn't in a bad enough state already.

PADDY. Who, man?

HUGHIE. The driver. (*Pause.*) Me oul' one, Paddy, the driver who . . .

PADDY. Aaaah. . . . Who crashed into her.

HUGHIE (*to* KILBY). A dirty fuckin' trick to play on someone. (*Pause.*) It's not on.

KILBY. Bit ungrateful, man . . .

HUGHIE. Yep. It's too much.

KILBY. . . . Aren't you?

HUGHIE. It's not fuckin' on, Kilby. Too much, you've gone *too* far. (*Pause.*)

KILBY. So, you didn't do it.

HUGHIE. No, I didn't. (*Long pause.*)

KILBY. That's bad, now. Took work, that. Detective work an' dog work. Puppacat did business for you . . .

HUGHIE. Puppacat did?

KILBY. . . . an' Puppacat doesn't do business. *Yeah,* the Puppa. But Kilby had foresight said, 'Fuckin', man. The fucker's no grace, he'll throw it back in your face, won't recognise it for the gesture it is'.

HUGHIE. I'm not throwin' an'thin' back fuckin' anywhere. I'm declinin' participation in Puppacat's fuckin' . . .

KILBY. *An'* Kilby.

HUGHIE. . . . You an' Puppacat's fuckin' surprise. (*Pause.*)

KILBY. You're declinin' participation.

HUGHIE. Much as I'm moved, man.

KILBY. Yeah?

HUGHIE. Touched as I am.

KILBY. Kilby stood back, man. Kilby observed. Puppa was the one smacked.

HUGHIE. What?!

KILBY. On the *head*, man. That's right. Dragged the fuck up to Bernie's, set up the Puppa-surprise. Surprise took time an' thought, took plannin' out of goodness, the benevolent Puppacat, magnanimous cunt *like* him, helpin' out his *man*. Givin' him justice an' payback an' the chance of some righteous batterin'.

HUGHIE. An' I 'preciate the gesture, man . . . You know? Respect to me, to me oul' one . . .

KILBY. Then why can't you accept it in good grace? Bit of bone breakin', fuckin' show you're grateful. 'Cos the Puppacat won't like it. Say that *now,* I will. Puppacat'll be upset, not to mention Kilby. May be some major tin star throwin' down, you know what I'm sayin'? (*Mimes throwing down star.*) Caution to the wind an' layin' fuckin' in. Be some Shotokan head stomps takin' place this particular night, this very address!

PADDY (*pause*). So did Bernie Denk not cripple the peg-leg?

KILBY. Everything *but,* man. 'Costed her, broke in, wrecked her gaff . . .

PADDY. Why?

KILBY. They're lovers. What d'you expect? They were lovers an' they had a tiff, she dumped him an' that's not the issue.

PADDY. An' why'd he wreck her gaff?

KILBY. 'Cos she dumped him, didn't I say?

PADDY. Why?

KILBY. He ca . . . (*Beat.*) Fuck off. He called her ma in the sack, all right? Now somethin's gonna have to . . .

PADDY. He *what?!*

KILBY. He called her ma! They were in . . . (*To* HUGHIE.) I'm not finished with you. (*To* PADDY.) They were in the sack saddlin' an' just as he was shootin' his muck in her . . .

PADDY. No way.

KILBY. . . . . He shouted it out. Yeah, freaked the peg-leg to fuck, an' peg-legs don't freak easy. Usually been through the mill when they get the fuckin' thing chopped off, they become impervious to *lesser* freakin's. Anyway, she dumped him, he hounded her, they made up an' all's lovey dovey again. They're doin' favours for Puppacat, so's he can do favours for you, Hughie, not that you give a fuck, throwin' it back in everyone's fuckin' face!!! (*Pause.*)

HUGHIE. You don't know what the fuck you're talkin' about. *You* understand, don't you, Paddy?

PADDY. Your reasons like?

HUGHIE. Yeah.

PADDY. Have to say, man.

KILBY. *Now!*

PADDY. . . . I don't see the problem.

KILBY. *Now,* man!!

HUGHIE. Your man didn't mean it, Paddy. For all we know it was me oul'one's fault, you know? She's an oul'one, she . . .

KILBY. Oul'ones don't crash, man. Oul'ones drive careful, fuckin' six miles an hour; check both sides 'fore fartin' . . . *an'* the fuckin' rear-view. It was his fault, man, piss positive.

HUGHIE. Kilby . . .

KILBY. So you're gonna have to go back up there.

HUGHIE. But . . .

KILBY. That's it, man, no. (*Short pause.*) The decision's made, the gavel is pounded. (*Long pause.*)

HUGHIE. Well, I'm not.

KILBY. Sorry?

HUGHIE. I'm not gonna, Kilby. (*Pause*.)

KILBY. Would that be in your dreams, now?

HUGHIE. No.

KILBY. Where'd it be?

HUGHIE. Be somewhere else.

KILBY. That right?

HUGHIE. Be in reality, man. I'm not fuckin' doin' it. (*Pause*.) It's me oul' one. D'you not understand? Oul' one, mother whose fuckin' . . . whose vagina I came out of, day one.

KILBY. I know where you came out of, man.

HUGHIE. Who bore me to fuckin' *term*, man, raised me up. Who wouldn't say feck 'stead of fuck, wouldn't even say flip. Have youse no concept of me torture, the loss I'm facin'?

KILBY. Potentially.

HUGHIE. . . . Of an'thin' beyond batterin'?! Fuckin' hell! (*Pause*.)

KILBY. Think I'll talk to Puppacat, get him to take *you* on, Paddy, huh? What d'you think? *This* touch-hole's on his way out.

HUGHIE. *I* am?

KILBY. Yeah.

HUGHIE. *You* are.

KILBY. On me way out?

HUGHIE. A touch-hole.

KILBY (*pause*). That's in there, now, Hughie. All right? That's carved on me brain, now, permanent. (*To* PADDY.) Paddy. (*To* HUGHIE.) Won't be forgotten. (*To* PADDY.) Paddy.

PADDY. What ?

KILBY. Get Puppacat to take *you* on, huh? (*Pause*.)

PADDY (*quietly*). Yeah.

HUGHIE. Fuck're you sayin' 'Yeah' for?

PADDY. Just . . . (*Short pause.*) *because,* man. I'm only . . .

HUGHIE. '*Yeah*', for fuck's sake?!!! (*To* KILBY.) An' Puppacat'd take him?!

KILBY. He might.

HUGHIE. His gee, man. Over me?! No offence, Paddy, but you couldn't hack it. (*To* KILBY.) What makes you think he could hack it?

KILBY. A hunch.

HUGHIE. A hunch?! A *guess,* man. (*To* PADDY.) No offence, Paddy . . . (*To* KILBY.) Guess of a *dirt*burger.

KILBY (*indicating his head*). I'm markin' all this in here, Hughie.

HUGHIE (*to* PADDY). An' when did you decide you wanted to work for Puppacat?!

KILBY. Did he say that?

PADDY. . . . I never said that.

KILBY. He said he *could.* (*Short pause.*)

PADDY (*to* KILBY). Well . . . You . . .

KILBY (*to* PADDY). I said. Fine! (*Beat.*) Did you agree, man?

PADDY. Yeah.

KILBY. Then you said too.

HUGHIE (*to* PADDY). On Kilby's hunch . . . ?! Guess ?! (*Beat.*) Paddy!

KILBY. *Hunch,* man.

HUGHIE. On Kilby's just decidin' out of the blue?!! (*Pause. To* KILBY.) What did you do while I was gone?

KILBY. Did nothin', man. Kilby was Kilby.

HUGHIE. A turkeyburger, yeah?

KILBY (*pause*). Bit of carvin' goin' on, Hughie. Touch-hole, dirtburger . . . On me brain, man. . . . Turkeyburger. 'Proachin' puppyness, gonna have to *be* one. Be a puppy, you won't like it. Paddy's not your man. Paddy's his own man. You don't dictate. (*To* PADDY.) Does he?

PADDY. No.

KILBY (*to* HUGHIE). See?

PADDY. But, same time, man, have to say, I'm not *against* you or an'thin. . . . You know? I'm not sidin' or an'thin', I'm wonderin'.

HUGHIE. Wonderin' what?

PADDY. Why you can't just do your job, man.

KILBY. 'Zactly.

PADDY. . . . Get it done. Don't get me wrong, man.

KILBY. Fuckin' 'zactly. (*Pause.*)

HUGHIE. Who the fuck are you to . . . ? No, wait, now.

PADDY. Hughie.

HUGHIE. . . . to fuckin' . . . Wait a sec. All a sudden, *you* . . . someone who never went out, broke a finger, let alone a pin or a head . . . are tellin' me . . . Am I hearin' this or what? . . . are tellin' me I can't do my job proper? (*Indicating* KILBY.) 'Cos this . . . ?

KILBY. Ah . . . ! Ah . . . !

HUGHIE. 'Cos this fuckin' . . . ?

KILBY. Ah . . . ! Don't say it. Have to pinch off your bronchis.

HUGHIE (*pause*). . . . 'Cos Kilby has a hunch?! You're tellin' me how to handle headbreakin', you can't even dress yourself, can you? Fuck sake, smackin' advice from someone . . .

PADDY. Don't . . . Hughie!

HUGHIE. . . . who wears . . .

PADDY. . . . Don't slag me fuckin' snorkel!!! (*Pause.*)

HUGHIE. . . . a filthy dirty, ugly, rubbish lookin' oul . . .

KILBY *grabs him by the throat.*

Urk!

KILBY. Don't slag Paddy's snorkel, man. You're slaggin' stools, you're slaggin' snorkels an' it's not fuckin' 'preciated. That thing has served him well an' faithful. Paddy?

PADDY. Ten years.

HUGHIE. Urk!

KILBY. It's kept him dry in the torrent, warm in the gale an' if you say any more, I won't just pinch off your bronchis, I'll tear out your gizzard. D'you understand? Just say 'Urk'.

HUGHIE. Urk!

> KILBY *lets him go. He falls to the floor clutching his throat and coughing.*

KILBY. Don't think the badge came off there, 'cos it didn't. That was controlled discipline, not mayhem. Badge comes off, you'll know it.

PADDY (*to* HUGHIE). Sorry, man.

KILBY (*to* PADDY). What're you . . . ? (*Sighs. Picks up* PADDY*'s video cassette.*)

PADDY (*to* HUGHIE). You all right?

KILBY. Can I borry this thing off you, Paddy?

PADDY. What? If you want.

KILBY. 'Cos I don't think we're gonna be watchin' it here, now. (*To* HUGHIE.) Hughie? Sorry I had to do that, man. (*Takes out nik-nax.*) Here, d'you want one? (*Holding packet out.*) They're *yours,* like. (*Pause.*) Don't be a little fuckin' sulk, now. I'll get you back for them. (*To* PADDY.) Paddy? Just one, now.

> PADDY *takes one.* KILBY *puts packet away.*

PADDY. You not havin' one?

KILBY (*holding up video cassette*). Savin' them.

> PADDY *puts nik-nak in his mouth. Sucks.*

> Bit in this where he . . . ? (*Remembers that* PADDY *is sucking.*) Oh. (*Short pause.*) Fuck it.

> KILBY *takes packet back out, has one himself. Sucks.* PADDY *begins chewing.*

PADDY. What're you sayin'? (*Remembers that* KILBY *is sucking.*) Oh.

> *Pause.* PADDY *waits.* KILBY *begins chewing.*

KILBY. Bit in this where he does his mad battle cry?

PADDY. Which one, man?

KILBY. What d'you mean?

PADDY. Does various.

KILBY. Does he?

PADDY. Yep. Various tones, frequencies . . .

KILBY. Hunky, man. They're funny noises he makes, aren't they?

PADDY. Mm.

KILBY. Funny but deadly, like. (*Putting on jacket. Pause.*) Just use your jacks 'fore I go, Hughie, yeah? Conclude me epic.

KILBY *exits.* HUGHIE *and* PADDY *looking at each other. Silence.*

HUGHIE. Paddy . . .

HUGHIE*'s pager goes off.*

PADDY. Who is it, man?

HUGHIE *looks at him.*

ACT TWO

The same. A week later. Daytime. KILBY *and* PADDY *enter,* PADDY *carrying an umbrella. Both are formally dressed, although* PADDY *still wears his snorkel. There are a few sandwiches on the table, several cans of lager. They proceed to take off jackets, etc.* PADDY *shakes out the umbrella.*

KILBY. That eight diagram shit's shit, man. That muck about scratchin' an eight with your pole durin' a ruckus. Figure eight on the floor? Bollox, man. An' a pole fighter never fights that flamboyant. Their movements're too wide, too circular. Suppose that looks good on film an' all, looks graceful, but real life it's short, jerky, straight lines; keep it tight in here, you know? Protect your body. That monk shit's just madness. An' you don't . . . Paddy!

PADDY *stops shaking umbrella.*

You don't just walk out of the temple like that either. You have to heft the urn, man, receive your tats. Well, not your tats . . .

PADDY. The urn ?

KILBY. . . . Your *brands.* Fuckin' giant urn blockin' the exit, man. Filled with white hot coals, have to heft it with your forearms like that; dragon an' tiger get branded in there.

PADDY. No way!

KILBY. . . . Seared in permanent. Yeah an' the fuckin' *pain,* Paddy.

PADDY. Yeah?

KILBY. 'Scrutiatin', 'parently.

PADDY. I'd imagine.

KILBY. So. You know . . . Bit lackin' in authentics.

PADDY. Mm. (*Short pause.*) Good, though.

KILBY. Oh, yeah. (*They sit down.*) Fuckin' excellent otherwise. (*Pause.*)

PADDY. What'd you think of Nancy an' Bernie?

KILBY. Fuckin' disgrace, man.

PADDY. Weren't they?

KILBY. The moans of her!

PADDY. *An'* him.

KILBY. What?

PADDY. Could hear it all the way 'cross the church. 'N'ah.'
Like that.

KILBY. Not '*N'ah*', man.

PADDY. What, then?

KILBY. '*Ma*', he was sayin'.

PADDY. Oh. (*Pause.*) She let him?

KILBY. They came to an agreement.

> KILBY *attacks* PADDY. PADDY *blocks and
> counterattacks, pulling his strike short.*

> On'y way he can get off, man.

PADDY. Jaysus! An' how'd she fall out of the pew?

KILBY. He put his hand in her nik-niks, man, cold paw on her
privates, she got a shock, jumped, wasn't wearin' her
fuckin' . . .

PADDY. Ah.

KILBY. . . . you know . . .

PADDY. . . . her prosthetic, right, so she'd nothin' to balance
her.

KILBY. Into the aisle, man, nik-niks exposed. I'd a great view;
purple, couple of stragglers.

PADDY. What?

KILBY. Pubes, man. Creepin ' out the side there like moss.

> KILBY *attacks.* PADDY *blocks and counterattacks, pulling
> his strike short.*

> Good stuff, Paddy.

PADDY. Yeah?

KILBY. You're blossomin'.

PADDY *attacks.* KILBY *blocks and counterattacks, hitting* PADDY *in the stomach, winding him.*

Sorry man. Shouldn't attack the Kilby like that. To strike back's me nature. You all right? To attack, to counterattack's Kilby's instinct. Get up there.

PADDY. I'm all right.

KILBY. Toughen you up anyway. What doesn't kill you. That right?

PADDY. Makes you stronger?

KILBY. That's right. Conditions you.

KILBY *goes over to window. Looks out. Pause.*

PADDY. C'mere, when you gonna show us you smashin' somethin' barehanded?

KILBY. When I've somethin' to smash.

PADDY. I'd love to see it.

KILBY. Somethin' worthy of me fist. Fuck is he, now? (*Pause. Looking out.*)

PADDY. I hate that fuckin' church.

KILBY (*moving away from window*). The steps, man?

PADDY. Thought I was gonna collapse.

KILBY. This is what I'm sayin' 'bout conditionin'. You need a regime.

PADDY. I mean . . .

KILBY. You listenin'?

PADDY. I *know* I do.

KILBY. I'll start you on one. Go on.

PADDY. . . . I mean, the on'y ones go to mass regular're fogeys an' how the fuck're they supposed to, every day of the week, you know, negotiate those . . . ?

KILBY (*going back over to window*). *I* don't know. Should find another church or somethin'. Stay at home. (*Short pause. Looking out.*) Fuck that fogey shit, man. Fuckin' *hate* them cunts.

PADDY. Why?

KILBY (*to himself*). . . . Fuckin' stinkholes! (*Beat. To* PADDY.) 'Cos they stink, man. (*Pause.*)

PADDY. C'mere. When Hughie comes up, right? Will you not mention an'thin 'bout me, you know . . .

KILBY (*coming away from window*). . . . Gettin' in there?

PADDY. . . . Joinin' the, yeah, the echelons. Wanna break it to him slowly; gentle. Wanna ease him the info. An' a day like today . . .

KILBY. I get you. Be wrong, would it?

PADDY. Be inappropriate. Solemn an' all's it is.

KILBY. It is, it's solemn. It's mournful.

PADDY. It is. Today's a day of support. (*Pause.*) Can't wait all the same, man. What d'you think he'll think?

KILBY. The Puppa?

PADDY. Of me, like.

KILBY. Be impressed, man. Big bloke such as yourself; strong, smart, vicious lookin' – don't smile – fuckin' capable . . . ? Don't smile 'front of him. I'll give you an attack, you defend. When he's here, like . . . Defend, do a technique, say nothin'. Might do it again, couple of times, put it in his head, 'Jesus, this fucker's good . . . '

PADDY. This *him*, now?

KILBY. ' . . . Good in the arts 'f he can counter the Kilby'. This is Puppacat.

PADDY. Right.

KILBY. What he's ponderin'. So be diligent.

PADDY. Vigilant. (*Beat.*) Diligent.

KILBY. Vigilant. No, you're right. Be ready. (*Pause.*)

PADDY. Why shouldn't I smile?

KILBY. Well, does he wanna see how nice you are? How sweet?

PADDY. No.

KILBY. What's he wanna see?

PADDY. How fuckin' . . . how vicious I am.

KILBY. That's right, so don't worry. You worried?

PADDY. A bit.

KILBY. Fuck that. (*Returning to the window.*) Be hunky monkey with me to vouch. Get you in now, get you workin', man . . .

PADDY. Hunky.

KILBY. . . . Get you a *wage.* (*Pause.*)

PADDY. Wasn't too happy, was he?

KILBY. Hughie?

PADDY. With Nancy an' Bernie.

KILBY. He wasn't. (*Short pause.*) Ah, sure. (*Beat.*) Kinda lightened it, though.

PADDY. Which? The . . .

KILBY (*simultaneous with 'the'*). The service. Gave it an element of levity.

PADDY. Did.

KILBY. . . . You think? As opposed to gravitas.

PADDY. Would you get up on her, Kilby?

KILBY. Nancy?

PADDY. Yeah.

KILBY. I *would,* yeah.

PADDY. D'you reckon it'd be hard with the stump an' all?

KILBY. Be like any other bird, man. Just grab a pawful of satchel an' pull your way in. I wouldn't run a *mile,* though.

PADDY. Ah no.

KILBY. . . . Or eat nik-nax out of her nik-niks. Or if I did I wouldn't suck them. But a jockey, now . . .

PADDY. 'Zactly.

KILBY. Good saddlin' for the experience of it. The novelty.

PADDY. Speakin' of nik-nax.

KILBY. Huh? Sure, have a sambo.

PADDY. Ah, fuck that.

KILBY. Not good enough now, that it? You fuck, see once you've had a taste . . .

PADDY. This is it, man. . . . You're hooked.

KILBY. See's he any, sure.

> PADDY *exits to kitchen.* KILBY *looks out window. Pause.*

Here he is now. (*Pause.*) Fuck's he holdin'?

PADDY (*off*). A brolly?

KILBY. *No!* Well, *yeah,* but . . .

PADDY (*entering*). None there, man.

KILBY. The fuck is he heftin'? (*Beat.*) Quick, man.

> PADDY *joins him at window.*

> (*To himself.*) Misses it . . . ?

PADDY. Where's he?

> *Buzzer sounds.*

KILBY. . . . 'Course. (*Buzzes* HUGHIE *in.*) There none?

PADDY. I'm gaggin', man.

KILBY. You junkie.

PADDY. I am. (*Short pause.*) The echelon junkie of nik-nak.

KILBY. Class, man.

PADDY. Yeah.

KILBY. Class-*ic*! 'Cos you *are* a fuckin' echelon.

> KILBY *attacks.* PADDY *blocks and counterattacks, pulling his strike short.*

An' a Fist of the Dragon to be.

PADDY. Sensei.

KILBY. Pupil.

> HUGHIE *enters, carrying an umbrella and Nancy's fake leg, wearing a suit.*

The fuck are you doin'?

HUGHIE (*taking off coat, etc*). Fuck her.

PADDY. That her prosthetic?

HUGHIE. Fuck *her* if she wants to heavy pet in church 'front of me dead oul'one. Huh? She wants to expose her dirty nana, fuckin' mockerize the ceremony, me time of mournin'. *Fuck* her. See how far she gets now.

KILBY. You didn't just rief it off her stump, did you?

HUGHIE. She left it down . . . No.

KILBY. Good.

HUGHIE. . . . an' I picked it up. Sittin' on Bernie Denk's lap, she'd her tongue in his gullet . . .

KILBY. Still?

HUGHIE. . . . fuckin', *yeah* still; tongue in his gullet, hand on his jockey, fuckin' prosthetic was left there, leanin' against the wall, so I sauntered by furtive, swiped it an' moseyed off. (*Sits down, fake leg on his lap.*) Price of lust, man.

PADDY. Mustn't've predicted that.

KILBY. Huh? She mustn't've.

HUGHIE (*to himself*). . . . Price of bein' a slut.

KILBY. Did you hear that, Hughie?

HUGHIE. I did.

KILBY. She mustn't've predicted that. (*To* PADDY.) Nice one, man.

HUGHIE (*coughs*). Fuck sake. (*Coughs. To* PADDY.) Think I got what you had, man.

KILBY. Bit of a tickle, yeah?

HUGHIE. More than a tickle, man. Bit of a bark.

PADDY. Mine's gone.

HUGHIE. Bit of a *hack* in me. *Top* of me fuckin' belly.

KILBY. Here's your keys. (*Throws them to* HUGHIE.)

HUGHIE (*catching them*). Puppacat not here yet?

KILBY. He should be. Probly doin' the usual . . .

PADDY. Chattin' . . .

KILBY. . . . thing, yeah. Givin' an audience. Was good all the same, Hughie.

PADDY. Wasn't it? Very poignant.

KILBY. Still. Better place, man.

PADDY. Where?

KILBY. Better place, Hughie. (*To* PADDY.) *Heaven,* you fuckin' . . .

PADDY. *Oh.*

KILBY. Fuckin' 'Where?'! (*To* HUGHIE.) An' what happened last time, man; shit done, gullet grippage an' all, shit said . . . ?

PADDY. That's right.

KILBY. Heat of the fuckin' moment, man. '*Course* there's understandin'. '*Course* there's respect. Sure, aren't we here to show that? Even Puppacat, busy an' all's he is, huh? takes time out? Come up, he will now, we'll have our private, our *echelon* wake. Little adios, send her on her way, you know?

HUGHIE (*pause*). She was good, she was.

KILBY. Your oul'one?

HUGHIE. Dolly, yeah.

KILBY. She was.

HUGHIE. Whatsay, Paddy? Bit of history there with yourself an' herself.

PADDY. *Lot* of history. Good times. Good days . . .

HUGHIE. The best of days.

KILBY. Dug me perm she did. Did I tell you that?

PADDY. Oul'ones love perms.

KILBY. So? Doesn't take from the compliment.

PADDY. No.

KILBY. . . . The intention.

HUGHIE. Many a time she gave Paddy his dinner.

PADDY. An' many a time I gobbled it up, fuckin' *licked* the plate.

HUGHIE. Didn't you?

PADDY. Licked it clean, man. Asked for more. 'Little Ollie Twist', she'd say.

KILBY. MORE?!!!

PADDY. 'Little Orphan Paddy', huh?

KILBY. MORE?!!!

PADDY. Never said that, Kilby. *Gave* you more 'cos she always had plenty. Growin' lads. That it, Hughie?

HUGHIE. Strappin' lads.

PADDY. That's it.

HUGHIE. An' that time you called up . . .

PADDY. Jaysus. Me complete nip, man.

KILBY. What?

PADDY. Was battered by the Knackers.

HUGHIE. Mugged. (*To* PADDY.) An' what did they take?

PADDY. Everything. Money, me wallet, me watch . . .

HUGHIE. . . . . your clothes . . .

PADDY. . . . . me shoes . . . Thought I was in for a rapin', I did. Your oul'one opens the door, clicks me there all cockadangle.

HUGHIE. What did she do, but?

PADDY. Took it in her stride, man. Sure it wasn't as if she'd never seen one in her time.

HUGHIE. No.

PADDY. . . . . was it? Your oul'fella's, your own . . .

HUGHIE. It wasn't.

PADDY. Took care of business, then. Jesus, bathed me wounds . . . Eye out to here, I had.

HUGHIE. . . . . Ran you a bath . . .

PADDY. Bubble bath. Fuckin' healin' salts, herbs, dose of
    Radox, the works; little bathrobe there, bit of talc . . .

HUGHIE. Good as fuckin' new, huh?

PADDY. Good as new.

HUGHIE. . . . Fuckin' woman! I'll miss her.

KILBY. We'll *all* miss her, man. (*Short pause.*) We'll all miss
    Dolly. (*Silence.*) You cryin'?

HUGHIE. No.

KILBY. It's all right to.

HUGHIE. I'm not.

KILBY. . . . 'F you're a faggot. That right, Paddy?

PADDY. Ah, Kilby!

KILBY. I'm messin', man.

PADDY. Cry if you want, Hughie.

HUGHIE. Nah, fuck that. (*Beat.*) Find me own time, you
    know? Mourn private. I will. Unhindered, unwatched . . .

PADDY. That's the best way, suppose. (*Silence.*)

HUGHIE. Ask you somethin', man?

KILBY. Go ahead.

HUGHIE. Am I out?

KILBY. What, of the echelons?

HUGHIE. Yeah. (*Pause.*) I am, amen't I.

KILBY. Dunno.

HUGHIE. Yeah, you know I am. (*Pause.*)

KILBY. We weren't gonna tell you 'til after.

HUGHIE. No, that's all right, man. That's hunky. (*Pause.*) New
    beginnin', huh? A life change, sure fuck it. (*Pause.*) Fuck it.

KILBY (*jumps*). *Jaysus!* (*Takes a pager off his hip.*)

PADDY. You got a beeper ?!

KILBY (*looking at it*). . . . Frightened the fuckin' . . . Down
    the Windsor. How much was yours, Hughie?

HUGHIE. Ten.

KILBY. You were robbed, man. Seven. Bargained him down, I did. (*Checks number.*) Puppacat. (*To* HUGHIE.) Bit of sellotape there, but it's perfect. Didn't even have to threaten a batterin'.

HUGHIE. Very good.

KILBY. Skills of the barter, man.

PADDY. Any nik-nax, Hughie?

KILBY. . . . Gift of the haggle. Know what I'm sayin'? Where's your fuckin' phone 'til I . . . ? (*Looking around.*)

PADDY. Hughie.

HUGHIE. What?

PADDY. Any nik-nax?

KILBY. . . . Only you haven't fuckin' . . . *Bollox!* The fuck's wrong with me? Have to go all the way, now, down the fuck . . . !

PADDY. Hughie.

KILBY. . . . the fuckin' . . . He's *none,* man!! (*Beat.*) Fuck sake. No *phone,* no . . .

PADDY. Mellow.

KILBY. . . . no *nik-nax* . . . I'm *in* me fuckin' mellow.

PADDY. Should've got yourself a mobile.

KILBY. What, an' be a melanoma head like the rest of them? (*To* HUGHIE.) There shops near here?

HUGHIE. On the corner.

KILBY. I'm no tool, Paddy.

PADDY. Get nik-nax.

KILBY. Maybe it's fuckin' nik-nax you want. Fuckin' 'mobile'! Where's the . . . ? (*Picks up umbrella.*) Be back in a minute.

HUGHIE. Take the keys with you.

KILBY. *Buzz* me in. (*Going to door.*) Lazy prick you!

KILBY *exits. Silence.*

PADDY. Mad cunt, isn't he ?

HUGHIE. Mm. (*Beat.*) Fuckim'!

PADDY. Huh ?

HUGHIE. Hear him commiseratin'? Fuckim'! Meets her once, you'd swear he knew her all his life, fuckin' fake. Talkin' 'bout understandin', fucksake, fuckin' respect as if he had any.

PADDY. He's plenty.

HUGHIE. What?

PADDY. Kilby's sensitive, man, you take the time, get some dialogue goin'. Fact, he's vulnerable, I'd say . . .

HUGHIE. Bollox.

PADDY. . . . insecure. Tellin' you, Hughie. All the fucker needs is patience, bit of understandin', whatever, you get *behind* the exterior, the mask, get the *real* Kilby. 'F people on'y made the effort . . .

HUGHIE. Fuck the effort.

PADDY. See?

HUGHIE. An' he didn't come here for the wake, Paddy, either. He came to see me expelled, the little satisfaction he'll get from it. (*Short pause.*) Betcha he hoped there'd be more, sure.

PADDY. More what ?

HUGHIE. Punishment, the fuck! Betcha he'd other plans for today. Betcha behind me back he was houndin' Puppacat, huh? Gimme a goodbye batterin'. 'Come on, the Pup, he deserves it.' Can just imagine the cunt.

PADDY. Well, what happened, man?

HUGHIE. Huh?

PADDY. To make him want to. It can't be just . . .

HUGHIE (*simultaneous with 'just'*). So he was?!

PADDY. He . . . Well, he . . .

HUGHIE. Doesn't fuckin' surprise me, Paddy. An' nothin' happened. 'Least nothin' I'm aware of. Maybe it's me threads, he's jealous? I don't know. . . . me style?

PADDY. I don't know.

HUGHIE. It's mutual, anycase. (*Beat*.) An' what did Puppacat say?

PADDY. Said 'No,' man. What d'you think?

HUGHIE. Did you see this?

PADDY. He told me.

HUGHIE. Well, fair play to Puppacat. Although, fuck it, fuck him, too. Fuckin' behaviour! (*Pause*.)

PADDY. How's your belly, man?

HUGHIE. The pains?

PADDY. Yeah.

HUGHIE. Bad. Worse than before. Fuck, before it was like grease in me grill, now when it comes it's like chip oil in a chip pan on full, man, you know that way? . . . Fuckin' *sears* me innards.

PADDY. Should see a doctor, man. Get some prognosis.

HUGHIE. Mm. (*Pause*.) The fuck d'*you* care?

PADDY. 'Course I care. I'm sorry what happened.

HUGHIE. Me oul'one?

PADDY. The echelons. Well, her as well, 'course, but . . .

HUGHIE. I bet you are. An' who's me replacement, I wonder, huh? Someone not too far? 'Sorry' me hoop! Some fuck name of Paddy?

PADDY. No.

HUGHIE. Don't 'No' me, man. You an' Kilby all coseyed up, now, couple of buds, sure what's the logical step? Petitionin' of Puppacat, I reckon. The lickin' of his hole, get you echeloned up. Am I right?

PADDY. Hughie, don't . . .

HUGHIE. Am I right?

PADDY. . . . don't . . . *Yes*, you're right, but don't start actin' all betrayed, man. This is *outside* you, *outside* us.

HUGHIE. No, it's not . . .

PADDY. It is.

HUGHIE. . . . it's *about* us. It's *all* about us. The fuck happened you, Paddy? (*Pause.*) Huh?

PADDY. I bloomed if you *must* know.

HUGHIE. You bloomed?!

PADDY. . . . Got out from, yeah, from under you an' blossomed. I stopped listenin' to you to me detriment, started listenin' to someone else to . . .

HUGHIE. Kilby?!

PADDY. . . . to me whatever. *Yeah,* Kilby.

HUGHIE. Advantage.

PADDY. . . . to me fuckin' advantage, man. Traded up, I did. Minion to echelon. 'Cos that's all I was with you. Keepin' me down all the time, fuckin' *stuntin'* me. You haven't a fuckin' clue what I'm capable of!!! (*Pause.*) All me fuckin' life!

HUGHIE (*pause*). What did the oul'one say that time you called up, Paddy?

PADDY. When?

HUGHIE. That time you were mugged, man, you called up nippy.

PADDY. Dunno.

HUGHIE. You do. 'F you remember what she did, then you remember what she said. Somethin' important. Somethin' we talked about since. (*Pause.* PADDY *shrugs.*) Paddy!

PADDY. Sorry, man.

HUGHIE. You fuckin' liar. You traitor.

PADDY. Traitor?!

HUGHIE. After all she fuckin' did for you. You're betrayin' her beliefs, man!

PADDY. An' what've you been doin' these past years?

HUGHIE (*short pause*). Ah, yeah, but . . .

PADDY. . . . Huh? Swear you never smacked in your life.

HUGHIE. . . . but have to tell you, man. Been ponderin' this *last* while. Realisin', re-evaluatin' . . . Somethin' happens, then, you know, a stressful, a cathartic . . . occurrence or couple of 'currences, you get a new perspective an' I've got one. What happened last week put a stamp on what I suspicioned, Paddy. Gave me sight to see me for what I've been an' those cunts for what they are.

PADDY. An' what are they?

HUGHIE. Cunts, man. Cunts to stay away from. Glad I'm out.

PADDY. Yeah, right!

HUGHIE. . . . Happy. No, I am, Paddy.

PADDY. Hang on. You spend . . .

HUGHIE. Didn't realise, but . . .

PADDY. . . . Wait now. (*Beat.*) You spend years tellin' me how great they are, how cool, then soon's . . .

HUGHIE. I know.

PADDY. . . . as . . .

HUGHIE. I fooled meself into thinkin' they were, *it was,* into believin', but the oul'one's kickin' clarified me perceptions an' I feel a need, now, to, I'm serious, a duty to caution you. All right? The last thing you wanna do is work for Puppacat. I could *tell* you shit. Shit that'd change your mind, man . . . right quick.

PADDY. So tell me.

HUGHIE. Can't.

PADDY. Yeah, right!

HUGHIE. Don't wanna get battered. That's *right,* right. Tell I'll get head smacked, so I'm . . . or fuckin' *worse,* man, so I'm not *gonna.* Suffice to say but. Shit you can't hack. Know what you can hack an' you can't hack this.

PADDY. An' why's that, now? 'Cos I don't polly up?

HUGHIE. Polly what?!

PADDY. . . . Like you, man? This isn't polly-polly land, Hughie. This is seat of your pants land an' pollyness is moot.

HUGHIE. Moot?

PADDY. . . . is a moot way of life, man. Live your life polly, you do, always have, *judge* things polly on a fuckin' . . . a polly-polly scale. Well I'm not on that scale. All right? That's not how you judge me any more. (*Short pause.*) Just 'cos I don't wear a Chief shirt, whatsis . . . ?

HUGHIE. John Rocha.

PADDY (*simultaneous with 'Rocha'*). . . . a John Rocha shirt like yourself, polly pants . . .

HUGHIE. *Trousers!*

PADDY. *Pants*, I says!! Or *any* of that polly shit, you think it fuckin' behoofs you to . . .

HUGHIE (*simultaneous with 'to'*). . . . Hoofs?

PADDY (*pause*). Huh?

HUGHIE. Think it *behoofs* me? Like a dunkey?

PADDY. Fuck is a dunkey?!

HUGHIE. I mean a . . .

PADDY. Fuckin' dunkey!

HUGHIE. . . . *a don*key. Fuckin' be*hoofs,* sure, fuck sake!

PADDY. An' I'll tell you what style is. *Guru* style. It's a durable dragon fist, a long lastin' snorkle . . .

HUGHIE. Dragon fist?

PADDY. . . . shit like that. (*Beat.*) The jacket, man! Kilby's jacket that Dolan stroked, you fuckin' . . .

HUGHIE *bends over in agony holding his stomach.*

. . . You know what I'm talkin' 'bout.

The intercom buzzes. HUGHIE *recovers, goes over to door, buzzes* KILBY *in, puts it on the latch. Pause.*

HUGHIE. Paddy.

PADDY. What?

HUGHIE. What did me oul'one say that time?

PADDY. I don't know.

HUGHIE. You do, you lyin' fuck! What'd she tell you, your hour of need?

PADDY. Hughie? Fuck your oul' one.

HUGHIE. What?!

PADDY. . . . An' fuck you. You heard me. You're out an' I'm in. It's over. I'm an echelon, you're not an' never the fuckin' twain, man. (*Beat.*) *Never* the twain.

KILBY *enters. Pause.*

What's the jack, man?

KILBY. I ever tell you about the tin star, Hughie? (*Approaching. In his face.*) When that's thrown down, I'm gonna scratch a jangle on you, take you over me *knee,* I'm gonna, an' break bits . . .

PADDY. What happened?

KILBY (*shouting*). . . . break them *choppin'.* (*To* PADDY.) What? Be another hour or so. We've to stall here 'til then.

HUGHIE *coughs.*

I better not catch that, Hughie. D'you hear me ?

HUGHIE. It's on'y a tickle, man.

KILBY. Tickle me hoop!

PADDY. Where is he?

KILBY. Down in James's Street, fuckin' . . .

PADDY. Hospital?

KILBY. . . . fuckin' yeah. Nancy's after havin' a mishap, havin' a tumble down steps, she's after. Steps of the Sacred Heart.

PADDY. How the fuck did . . . ?

KILBY. She's missin' a leg, Paddy.

HUGHIE. Fuck her.

PADDY. But was she not . . . ?

KILBY (*to* HUGHIE). *Fuck* her?! (*To* PADDY.) Not what? (*To* HUGHIE.) That's lovely.

PADDY. . . . watchin' what she was doin'.

KILBY (*to* HUGHIE). . . . So *considerate,* man. (*To* PADDY.)
She was upset, Paddy. Her attention was on other things.

HUGHIE. Like what? Bernie Denk's flute?

KILBY. Funny, man. How 'bout a five grand prosthetic?

PADDY (*of leg*). That?!

KILBY. . . . she thought was gone forever. Could be more,
Paddy. Tried to get her to calm down, they did. Tried to get
her to *sit* down, but she insisted on standin', hoppin',
weaker sex shit, fuckin' wailin' an' all, 'I'm gonna have to
save for a new one!' Hysterical. 'It's gonna take me years!'
She didn't see, hoppin' backwards, the top step . . . pogoed
off the edge an' down she tumbled. Thirty-six of the
concrete fuckers. *Steep* fuckers. Head over hogans, she
went, smacked damagous off each an' every one.

HUGHIE. For someone can see the future, she's not very good
at . . . fuckin' seein' the future.

PADDY. *I* said that, man.

KILBY. So what we do is . . . He fuckin' did *too.*

PADDY. *What* do we do?

KILBY. . . . Cheatin' cunt, you. (*To* PADDY.) We stall. (*To*
HUGHIE.) Said to tell you, man . . .

PADDY. Stall?!

KILBY. That too difficult?

PADDY. No.

KILBY. Cunt strokin' your gags, man, huh? (*To* HUGHIE.)
Said to tell you it *was* on'y gonna be a talk, man. You an'
Puppacat jaw-jigglin', him expellin' you verbal. Asked me
to relay to you, he did, inform you it's gone up, now, 'cos
of your boldness. Now he's expellin' you *corporal* 's gonna
snap bones various an' sundry.

HUGHIE. Himself ?

KILBY. He's bringin' her true love to avenge her on you. Bernie
Denk up to do what he will in his grief. Purgin' an' shit, you
know? Says you're fucked 'cos he's gonna give Bernie free
rein, an' distraught an' frenzied's he's gonna be . . .

HUGHIE. Motherfucker.

KILBY. An' he is, man.

HUGHIE. What?

KILBY. He *did* fuck his mother.

HUGHIE. I'm talkin' 'bout Puppacat, not Bernie. (*Short pause.*) Cunt, *like* him.

KILBY. Shut the fuck up.

HUGHIE. Fuckin' mule!

KILBY. . . . You hear me?

HUGHIE. Make me. (*Pause.*)

KILBY. I will if you test me. Tin badge comes off, then . . .

HUGHIE. Sure you're allowed?

KILBY. . . . then . . . What?

HUGHIE. Don't think you're allowed, some reason.

KILBY (*pause*). Paddy. Somethin' you're gonna have to learn. All right? Keep your fuckin' mouth shut.

> KILBY *attacks for real.* PADDY *defends and counterattacks, pulling his strike short. Pause.*

You fuckin' with me?

PADDY. No, man.

KILBY. Huh?

PADDY. That was instinct. (*Pause.*)

KILBY. The apprentice learns fast.

PADDY. Well . . .

KILBY. Paddy. Textbook.

PADDY. Cheers.

KILBY. Proud of you. (*Gives* HUGHIE *a slap.*) Wasn't let *then,* Hughie. When Paddy told you, I wasn't. But *now*, maybe the situation's changed. Maybe I'm let give you a warmer upper like your man mangled your oul'one was warmed up, brass knucks an' broken teeth. You 'member? Maybe that's Kilby's instructions.

PADDY. *Is* it, man?

KILBY. Huh? 'Fraid not, Paddy, no. Can't slap major, much to
me fuckin' . . . chagrin. Though get ready yourself, man,
yeah? Do your share if the Puppa demands it.

PADDY. Of batterin'?

KILBY. 'Cos he might.

PADDY (*pause*). How bad'll it be?

KILBY. Dunno. Stand you good stead, but.

PADDY. Bad, but?

KILBY. Depends on Puppacat, man. On Bernie. I'd imagine
bad, yeah. You on? I *hope* bad. You on?

PADDY. Well . . .

KILBY. 'Course you are. This'll be your chance, see. Your
audition piece. Audition for Puppacat, demo first hand in
person, man, your focused viciousness, willin'ness to
inflict. You with me? Get you in this very day. I want you,
he'll say. I want Kilby's apprentice paid a wage. Steve
Lynch owes me money, needs a smackin'. Send the deputy
sheriff of crip, man, his sidekick, the nik-nak kid. Am I
right?

PADDY. The nik-nak kid.

KILBY. Am I learnin'?

PADDY. You are.

KILBY. Here. (*Throws him nik-nax.*)

PADDY. Oh, *wild*, man !

KILBY. Who's that fuck? They'll say. Think I'd leave you
without?

PADDY *begins sucking and chewing.*

Who's that fuck with the Kilby, swaggerin' all cocky an'
earnin' himself a rep? I hear he likes the nik-nax, they'll
say. In nik-nax as it is in batterin', I hear. As it is in his
victims. Sucks them dry, then crunches, chews them. That
right, Paddy? . . . swallies them down. That right, man?

PADDY (*sucking a nik-nak*). Mm?

KILBY (*to* HUGHIE). Fuckin' loves the nik-nax.

PADDY (*begins chewing*). D'you want one?

KILBY. Nah, man. Paddy an' Kilby, partners bonded, tin badges unclipped an' woe betide they don't get thrown down, huh? Woe betide the non-echelon. Ah, sure, go on. (*He takes some nik-nax.*) 'Cos there'll be double the reckonin'. Won't there?

PADDY. There will.

KILBY. Reckonin' times two, man.

> KILBY *puts nik-nax in his mouth. He and* PADDY *suck six or seven seconds, then chew.*

> Mm.

PADDY. Yeah.

KILBY (*to* HUGHIE). Where's your keys?

HUGHIE. There.

KILBY. Feel a bohoemoth brewin'.

> *He grabs the keys, goes over to door and locks it, puts them in his pocket.*

> (*To* PADDY.) So's he doesn't bolt, see.

HUGHIE. Wasn't *gonna* bolt.

KILBY. Have to empty me gulley trap.

> KILBY *exits to toilet. Pause.* HUGHIE *stands up, goes over to* KILBY*'s jacket.*

HUGHIE. So, Paddy's made his choice, yeah?

PADDY. Yeah.

HUGHIE. Even though Hughie's in peril. Fair enough, man.

PADDY. Just doin' me job.

HUGHIE. Fair enough. (*Bringing* KILBY*'s jacket to* PADDY.) Have a look at that. (*Shows him inside label.*) That familiar?

PADDY. Which?

HUGHIE. The writin'. That say Dragon Fist?

PADDY (*reading*). 'Dry clean only as . . . '

HUGHIE. The chink, man!

PADDY (*reads. Pause*). Made in China.

HUGHIE. How sage is that? Huh? (*Hanging jacket back up*.)
Copies it off the label. How fuckin' guru is that? An' sells it
to CopperDolan? '*Nother* fuckin' chunkhead.

PADDY. He told me he stroked it.

KILBY *enters*.

KILBY. You've no fuckin' jacks roll, Hughie.

HUGHIE *searches*.

(*To* PADDY.) Squattin' there, spotted man. Gettin' ready for
me first heave, fuckin' perceived. Fuck's wrong with you?

PADDY. Nothin'.

KILBY. . . . Huh? There fuckin' *is*.

Pause. HUGHIE *stops searching*.

PADDY. You told me it said Dragon Fist.

KILBY. What did?

PADDY. Your jacket.

KILBY. That's what it *does* fuckin' . . . (*Pause. To* HUGHIE.)
You low stoopin' supergrass, Hughie. Know what that's
gonna get you?

HUGHIE. Nothin' I'm not already gettin'.

KILBY. Says whatever I want it to say, Paddy. That's the best
thing '*bout* chink writin'.

HUGHIE. Not to some people, man. Not to CopperDolan.

KILBY. Where's your jacks roll? An' shut the fuck up!!!

HUGHIE. None left.

KILBY. Well, tissues, then! Fuckin' kitchen roll! C'mon, you
cunt, I'm burstin'!

PADDY. What'd CopperDolan do?

KILBY. Nothin'.

HUGHIE. But Puppacat, now. Huh? What your boss to *be*
did . . .

PADDY. *What'd* he do?

HUGHIE. . . . to the little Kilby. What'd he *do,* man?! (*Looks at* KILBY. *Long pause.*) Gonna tell your legend.

KILBY. You're dead, man.

HUGHIE. . . . Tell it to Paddy. Dead *any* case.

KILBY. By *me,* but.

HUGHIE. That right?

KILBY. . . . By the Kilby. You tell him, man . . .

PADDY. Sure, fuck it.

KILBY. . . . an' I'll . . . What?

PADDY. I don't wanna know.

KILBY. Ah, no, Paddy. No. Hughie'll tell you an' you know what I'll do to him? (*To* HUGHIE.) You know what I'll fuckin' do to you?!! I'll fuckin' . . . I'll . . . Where's your fuckin' jacks roll?!!! (*To* PADDY.) Paddy. Find me tissues. (*To* HUGHIE.) After me fuckin' shite!

KILBY *exits.* PADDY *begins searching for tissues.*

HUGHIE (*pause*). See, CopperDolan saw the writin' there, Paddy, thought it looked alpha. An' it *did* look alpha. Fuckin' *stitch*work? (*Appreciative whistle.*) Stool boy in there . . .

PADDY. Who?

HUGHIE. Stool . . . Scutter boy. (PADDY *stops searching. Short pause.*) Kilby, man. The fuck's he doin'?

PADDY. Takin' a shit. (*Beat.*) Ah . . .

HUGHIE. . . . was short of cash, okay? Needed money, send away the states for these jeans. Don't know if . . .

PADDY. He did.

HUGHIE. His Chuck jeans?

PADDY. With the gusset.

HUGHIE. . . . Needed money, so they bartered a bit; hundred, hundred an' twenty-five, Kilby needed two-fifty so he told CopperDolan it said, the *writin'* like, said Brotherhood of the Guard, hiked the fuckin' . . .

PADDY. Brotherhood of . . . ?

HUGHIE. *Gards*, man. D'you get it?

PADDY. Coppers.

HUGHIE. . . . Hiked the price up. 'Zactly. Told him he could impress them all down the Gook Nation, as if he wouldn't find out eventually. Huh? As if the chinks couldn't read what the chink writin' writ. An' that's the fuck you wanna folly, wanna be your Yoda in batterin'?

PADDY. So, what happened?

HUGHIE. D'you get that fuckin' stink? Phew!

PADDY (*beat*). I . . .

HUGHIE. Don't tell me you don't, now.

PADDY. I *do*! (*Beat.*) Fuck sake!

HUGHIE. How many shites did he have the other night?

PADDY. Three. One.

HUGHIE. Three or one?

HUGHIE. One. They were three parts of the same shite.

HUGHIE. No they weren't, they were separate.

PADDY. Fine. What did CopperDolan do?

HUGHIE. Dolan did nothin'. *Puppacat,* but.

PADDY. Well, what did *Puppacat* do?!

HUGHIE (*pause*). *Caused* that stink.

KILBY (*off*). Hughie!

HUGHIE. One day, see, Dolan's down Delgado's havin' his billy club sucked by Minnie Pearl P'au . . . You know Minnie?

KILBY (*off*). Paddy!

PADDY. No.

HUGHIE. Call her the Yellow Pearl.

PADDY. Don't know her, man.

KILBY (*off*). You fuckin' deaf?!

PADDY (*shouting*). What?!!

KILBY (*off*). C'mon with the fuckin' tissues!

PADDY. Hang on!!

HUGHIE. Gook bird down Delgado's. Hooer, like.

KILBY (*off*). I *won't* hang on.

HUGHIE. . . . CopperDolan blows muck in her gob after sayin' he wouldn't, she goes apeshit, right? 'Cos he's done it before many a time an' she's sick of it, can't abide the taste of fuckin' paste. Minnie reveals somethin' in her wrath this night, somethin' many a gook knows, an' *has* known, but few gooks'll say for fear of Copper*Dolan's* wrath. That what he's been wearin' proud, struttin' all boastful an' thinks says Brotherhood of the Guard actually says . . .

PADDY. Right.

HUGHIE. . . . Made in China.

PADDY. I fuckin' adored that jacket.

HUGHIE. So poor CopperDolan, mockery of gooks all over, loses face, so, see, loses honour, the place of his beat, needs somethin' to restore it. Meantime. His boys an' the echelons're about to make their deal . . .

KILBY (*off*). I'll fuckin' burst you, paddy!!

HUGHIE. . . . The Parish Treaty, on'y . . .

PADDY (*shouting. To* KILBY). I'm lookin'!

HUGHIE. . . . On'y the jacket embarrassment's queerin' things up. All right? CopperDolan wants a certain thing done 'fore he'll commit.

PADDY. What's that? Come on.

HUGHIE. . . . An' Puppacat needs him to commit. Hang on.

PADDY. Hughie!

HUGHIE. . . . I'm gettin' there. Wants somethin' done by Puppacat, show he's sorry. Wants some kind of punishment meted out to Kilby, give him satisfaction. Otherwise it's not gonna happen. Echelons'll end up bein' the lower 'stead of the higher. So we all meet down Delgado's this night, night of the treaty; CopperDolan, few goons, Puppacat, meself, couple of echelons. Puppacat gives the nod – I'm nearly finished, man – gives the nod, we all go for Kilby. Echelons *an'* goons. An' adept an' all's he is at the arts, now, skilled 's he *is* – Got a whack or two meself – we grab an' restrain him . . .

PADDY. You helped?!

HUGHIE. I had to. . . . bend him over table six . . . I was ordered, man, sure. Same's you'll be. Puppacat leans down an' looks him in the eye, man, says, I'll never forget, says, 'I'll make this up to you, Kilby'. Then another nod an' we rief, as per Puppacat's instructions, down Kilby's strides, tear *off* his understrides. Puppacat goes up behind him, fuckin' pool cue in his paw, there, hefts, holds it, gives the end an oul' chalkin' an' . . .

PADDY. Oh, Jaysus!

HUGHIE. . . . Yep . . .

PADDY. Up his dirty dirt road?!!!

HUGHIE. 'Bout two fuckin' *foot* up his dirty dirt road.

PADDY. Ah, *fuck!*

HUGHIE. *Three* foot, maybe.

PADDY. *Fuck,* man! He never told me this shit.

HUGHIE. Well, he wouldn't.

PADDY. . . . This horrid shit. *Fuck,* an' his own boss?!

KILBY *enters and sits down.*

HUGHIE. *Your* boss to *be*, man. (*To* PADDY.) Welters of gore, there was, fuckin' *geysers* of blood spurtin', *sprayin'* out of both ends of him, hole *an'* mouth. That right, Kilby? Gurglin' like a blocked drain.

PADDY. Jesus Christ!

HUGHIE (*to* KILBY). Speakin' of blocked drains. (*To* PADDY.) I *know,* man. (*To* KILBY.) You never hear of flushin'?

KILBY. I'm enjoyin' me bouquet.

HUGHIE. Your . . .

KILBY. Bouquet of me creation. (*Inhales deeply.*) Relishin', I am.

HUGHIE. Fuck sake! (*On his way out.*) An' how the fuck did you wipe your hole?

KILBY. Clothes in your basket.

HUGHIE (*in doorway. Beat*). What?! (*Runs out.*)

KILBY. Strips of John Rocha.

HUGHIE (*off, shouting*). Oh, you cunt!!!

KILBY. A smooth moppin' of crevice.

HUGHIE (*off, shouting*). You dirty, dirty cunt!!! (*Silence.*)

PADDY. Kilby?

HUGHIE (*off, shouting*). You fuckin' scumbag!!!

PADDY. Have to say, man . . .

KILBY (*of* HUGHIE). You hear this?

PADDY. . . . All this new shit, you know? I do.

KILBY. Desired effect.

PADDY. What he just told us, man? Kinda givin' me pause, it is.

KILBY. Fuck're you talkin' 'bout?

PADDY. Pause for thought, man. Think I might leave it for today, catch Puppacat again, I think, whatsay? Do the oul' technique thing an' all the next time, huh? Reckon I need to mull a bit if you know what I'm sayin'. On this info, like. (*Pause.*) So will you open the door for us?

KILBY. You're not gonna join, you fuck, are you? Now that you've . . .

PADDY. No, man, I am. Fuck. Just the situation's not what I thought it was before, so I can't lep into it lightly.

KILBY. Stay, man.

PADDY. . . . Have to *look* before I lep. 'Fer not to, Kilby. 'Fer not to, will you give us the key? 'Fer to split, so will you give us it?

KILBY (*pause*). Gonna keep you here a while, watch Kilby get personal with Hughie.

PADDY. But . . .

KILBY. . . . All right? Dance a tango, think you follow. No, you're part of this now. Fucker's no business.

PADDY. An' what about Puppacat?

KILBY. . . . None a'tall! What?

PADDY. . . . An' Bernie. You're not allowed touch him 'til . . .

KILBY. *Wasn't,* Paddy. *Wasn't.* But the release of that story's justification, man. D'you not think? . . . Is a personal attack on me an' Puppacat, gives me sanction as the deputy sheriff to supersede the avengin' of Nancy by Bernie. An' I'll leave him the dregs, like.

PADDY. Well, fair enough, man. 'Fer to leave it *to* you, but. Whatsay? Just eh . . . retreat. You know? 'Vaporate . . .

KILBY. Paddy . . .

PADDY. . . . Come back when the aggro's over.

KILBY. . . . Paddy. Sit down an' have a nik-nak. Give us one.

PADDY *gives him one.*

Gonna sit here, all right ? Sit down !

PADDY *sits.*

Gonna suck. (*Sucks five or six seconds.*) Mmm. Chew. Swally. (*Takes chewed up nik-nak from mouth.*) *Not* swally, should say. (*Puts it on table.*) Recline back an' *wait,* should say.

PADDY. Right.

KILBY. . . . Cultivate me rage.

The toilet flushes.

PADDY. But, listen . . .

KILBY. D'you hear me? Me fuckin' *rage!*

HUGHIE *enters with John Rocha shirt.*

HUGHIE. Been cultivatin' mine as well, man. So, Paddy, so . . .

KILBY. How's the shirt?

HUGHIE. . . . the cue stick did . . . (*To* KILBY.) *Wrecked,* you cunt! (*To* PADDY.) . . . did damage up there, see . . . (*To* KILBY.) You destructive *cunt!!* (*To* PADDY.) Whenever an'thin' not veg or fruit enters his body it sets off his bowels, 's you can see. (*Holds out shirt.*) He becomes incapable of clutchin' his filth. (*Dumps shirt in bin. To* KILBY.) Don't you. (*To* PADDY.) Doesn't usually stray from the veg, but . . .

KILBY. Couldn't resist the oul' Nik-Nax . . .

HUGHIE. . . . could you?

HUGHIE *sits down.* KILBY *stands up.*

KILBY. Not the rib n' saucys.

HUGHIE *stands up.*

What're you standin' up for?

HUGHIE (*backing away*). Readiness.

KILBY (*approaching*). What're you backin' up for?

HUGHIE. Tactics.

KILBY. Retreatin'?

HUGHIE. Manoueverin'.

They circle the room. KILBY *advancing,* HUGHIE *retreating. Continue this until stated.*

KILBY. Me rage is up there, Hughie. The highest of planes.

HUGHIE. So's mine, man. (*To* PADDY.) So Puppacat's finished rootin', Paddy. (*To* KILBY.) Just to wrap up. (*To* PADDY.) . . . He takes the cue stick back out . . . You listenin'?

PADDY. Yeah.

HUGHIE. . . . Kilby's hole an' he's not too, what's the word? Lucid. So, there's all fuckin' stuff on it, an' Kilby says, 'What the fuck is that?!' You know? Asks what all this muck on the cue stick is. Guess what Puppacat says? (*Short pause.*) Paddy!

PADDY. What?

HUGHIE. It's your shite an' your guts. An' you'd wanna hear CopperDolan.

KILBY. C'mon.

HUGHIE. . . . The guffaws of him.

HUGHIE does CopperDolan's laugh.

KILBY. You're wastin' time.

HUGHIE. I'm bidin' time.

Does CopperDolan's laugh.

KILBY. An' that's not how he guffaws.

HUGHIE. How, then?

KILBY. Not tellin' you.

HUGHIE. It's your shite an' your guts, Paddy. Then he . . .

KILBY does CopperDolan's laugh; angrily.

That's not fuckin' it. (*To* PADDY.) Then CopperDolan puts his right hand in it, smears it all over, gives Puppacat a little look like that. Kinda sly an' evil, not to be biblical, now, Puppacat does the same an' they shake . . .

PADDY (*to* KILBY). In your shite?

KILBY. Huh?

PADDY. They shook in your shite?!

KILBY. Shook symbolic, they did, all ceremonial, made the pact legit an' bindin' on the sufferin', the martyrdom of Kilby. An' that *is* his fuckin' guffaw!

HUGHIE. I pre . . .

KILBY does CopperDolan's laugh; very angrily.

I presume that's why he hates me. (*To* KILBY.) Is it? (*To* PADDY.) 'Cos I was witness to his shame.

KILBY. Because you helped, you fuck!

HUGHIE. I was ordered.

KILBY. You could've said no, man! (*Pause.*) Or . . .

HUGHIE. Kilby comes out of a coma three days later . . . This right, man? This bit true?

KILBY. What?

HUGHIE. You woke up an' you'd a perm?

KILBY *stops advancing. Pause.*

Ordeal harrowed your hair up so curly no-one can straighten it, you've gone to everyone in town, keeps curlin' back?

Pause. HUGHIE *has manouevered himself in front of the baseball bat.*

KILBY. That's a real fuckin' paid for perm, man, groomed an' styled an' you're a liar. You're an insidious little fuck, have to conquer with lies an' shitstirrin'. The badge is down now, you hear me? (*Mimes throwing down badge.*) The tin star is well an' truly on the floor an' Kilby's fuckin' ragin'!! Ragin' like a beast an' ready to fuckin' maim!!!

KILBY *attacks.* HUGHIE *picks up the baseball bat and hits him in the arm.*

HUGHIE. C'mon, then, you permy fuck, you.

They circle.

KILBY. I'll let you have that one, Hughie.

HUGHIE. Which? The whack? Or . . .

KILBY. The whack, man.

HUGHIE *feints.*

The whack I'll grant you. The perm comment's another fuckin' tale.

HUGHIE *feints.*

Not one more blow'll penetrate me defences. (*Pause.*) Ready for you, I am.

HUGHIE *feints.*

Me mind is focused. (*Short pause.*) Me wrath is channelled. (*Pause.*) Gonna inflict.

HUGHIE *attacks,* KILBY *on the defensive, avoiding strikes with skill, before knocking the bat out of* HUGHIE*'s hands. Pause. Circling.* KILBY *throws a less than waist high side kick.* HUGHIE *dodges it easily.* KILBY *tries again with a roundhouse kick. This too is less than waist high and easily dodged by* HUGHIE.

The fuck? Where the fuck's me high leg action? (*Tries a spinning back kick with the same result.*) These fuckin' . . . See this, Paddy?

HUGHIE *picks up Nancy's fake leg.*

'F I had me Chucks, now, bollox! Me action jeans.

HUGHIE *gives the distracted* KILBY *a whack with the leg, dropping him.*

HUGHIE (*ready to strike again*). You lackin' your gusset, Kilby?

KILBY. Ah! Ah! Don't! (*Pause.*) Don't fuckin' use that. That's five grand's worth of prosthetic, man. That's Nancy's fuckin' savin's. Don't break it. (*Pause*). Think of *her,* Hughie. (*Pause.*) Think of poor Nancy, 'spite of her faults, man. (*Pause.*)

HUGHIE. Fuck Nancy.

HUGHIE *raises the leg again to strike, but suddenly lets out a howl, drops the leg and doubles over, holding his stomach.*

Aagh! Fuck! Fuck!

KILBY *gets up and grabs him.*

KILBY. Need some medicine, do you? (*Getting behind him.*) Take your pick man. (*Punches him in ribs with left.*) Castor oil? (*Punches him in ribs with right.*) . . . Or milk of magnesia? You fuckin' muckhole, you. Paddy! (*Picking up umbrella.*) Get over here, do me a job. Take this brolly.

PADDY. Ah, you're all right, man.

KILBY (*looks at* PADDY. *Pause*). I fuckin' *know* I'm all right. C'mon. Want you to expand the girdle of Hughie's ringpiece. (*To* HUGHIE.) Take your trousers off.

HUGHIE. Me hole!

KILBY. That's what I'm tryin' to get to, man. Take them off, save me boxin' your head to get them off. (*To* PADDY.) Paddy! (*To* HUGHIE.) Gonna show you what it's like to be a cue stick's whore. (*To* PADDY.) C'mon, man. Bit of impalin'. Well within your powers.

PADDY. Em . . .

KILBY. . . . Your skills. I'll hold him for you. All you've to do is press it against the pink little star an' thrust. (*Pause.*) *C'mooooon!!!* Sober dialogue, Paddy, you don't. Now, get over here 'fore I scold you.

PADDY *approaches.*

Good man. (*Gets* HUGHIE *into a one-handed arm lock.*) See this lock, man?

PADDY *picks up baseball bat.*

Incapacitate your opponent single pawed, leaves the other free for whatever you want. (*Opening* HUGHIE*'s belt. Pulling down his trousers.*) It's popular with faggot rapists an' berserk sodomites. (*Slaps* HUGHIE*'s arse.*) Bit of a slap, there, Hughie, shame you. You like that? (*Slaps his arse.*) You ashamed? (*Slaps his arse.*)

PADDY. Kilby!

KILBY. Just relax the oul' sphincter, now. Don't clench, man, be easier for one an' all. (*Holds umbrella out.*) You right, Paddy, here. You know where to aim. (*Pause.*) Will you *take* the fuckin' . . . !!!

PADDY *whacks him over the head with the baseball bat.*

Oh! Oh, good fuck! (*Reeling, dropping umbrella.*) I'm all dizzy an' all.

PADDY. Fuck that buggerin' shit.

KILBY. You knocked me for six. The fuck's wrong with you? After skullhaulin' me, you are. Gimme that bat.

PADDY. Gimme the keys.

KILBY (*approaching*). I'll take it off you.

PADDY. Gimme the fuckin' keys so's I can get the fuck . . .

HUGHIE. Paddy!

PADDY. . . . *out* of here !!!

KILBY *makes for Nancy's leg.*

HUGHIE. He's goin' for the fuckin . . . !!!

HUGHIE *goes for the leg himself, trips over his trousers, falls on his face.*

Ouch!

KILBY (*picking the leg up*). Out on your snot, Hughie.

PADDY. You all right, man?

HUGHIE. Fuck !

Over following, HUGHIE *gets back up and pulls up his trousers, buttons them, etc.*

KILBY. So come on, Paddy.

KILBY *and* PADDY *circle.*

See if you can get your keys off the Kilby.

PADDY. I'll beat you down.

KILBY. Not in me fury, man. Gonna . . .

HUGHIE (*standing with the umbrella in his hands*). Kilby . . .

KILBY. . . . Gonna nab you, I am. (*Sees* HUGHIE.) Oh.

HUGHIE. That's right.

HUGHIE *and* PADDY *circle* KILBY. *All three have their weapons raised.*

KILBY. Two against one.

HUGHIE. That's right. Drop the prosthetic.

KILBY. . . . I like the odds.

HUGHIE. Drop the prosthetic or we'll pound down upon you, Kilby!!!

They continue to circle. KILBY *looks at* HUGHIE. *Looks at* PADDY. *Pause.*

KILBY. Pound ahead.

They engage. After several exchanges, KILBY *having the upper hand, they stop and circle,* KILBY *spinning the leg above his head.*

Think youse can duel me? Youse're rubbish, man. Can youse not feel me ease?

HUGHIE *coughs.*

No? Feel me toyin' with youse all devil-may-care?

HUGHIE. Prosthetic as pole.

KILBY. That's right, man.

HUGHIE. Very MacGuyver.

PADDY. Pole's your weapon of choice.

KILBY. That's right. Feel me nonchalance, now?

Pause. They continue to circle. HUGHIE *coughing.*

Attained a knowin' state that day, I did, day I was impaled.
Somethin' youse cunts'll never understand. Mastery was
attained; understandin', balance . . . State a monk of Shaolin
reaches when he lifts that giant urn, you get me, Paddy?
When he brands himself in white fire; the torment, the pain,
I reached that state. Bear the marks, I do. Damage to me
bowels within, the curls on me head without. They're *my*
dragon an' tiger, see, 'cos I *am* Shaolin. I'm the treaty, I'm
echelon incarnate.

HUGHIE *coughing.*

I am alpha male of youse fucks 'cos I can take it an' have
took it to the fuckin' hilt, man. Youse're on'y twopenny
strong, twopenny true. Your convictions're twopenny. I took
cue stick . . .

HUGHIE *coughing.*

I took . . .

HUGHIE *coughing.*

Shut the fuck up!! Fuckin' barkin' like a mutt! I took
fuckin' . . .

PADDY. Some Venos, Hughie.

KILBY. 'Zactly. The fuck was I . . . ?

PADDY. . . . Sort you right quick.

KILBY. I took cue stick stoic an' acceptin' an' me will was
forged tenfold stronger in, yep, in shite an' guts! Thick, ripe
shite, too. Black shite. Your will's forged in piss, man, the
pair of youse. Weak fuckin' watery piss, not even yellow,
an' that's why youse'll never beat me. (*Short pause.*) Gonna
take you out first, Hughie, hew a gorge in you.

KILBY *feints at* PADDY. PADDY *jumps back.*

Youse ready to re-engage?

KILBY *feints at* PADDY. PADDY *jumps back.*

You jumpy cunt, you, Paddy.

PADDY. Kilby.

KILBY (*spinning leg*). Youse ready, now?

PADDY. Don't be mayhemic.

KILBY. Let's go, then.

> KILBY *attacks. They fight.* KILBY *hits* PADDY *in the leg, dropping him with a scream.* KILBY *versus* HUGHIE. *A short exchange, followed by a vicious pummelling from* KILBY. HUGHIE *drops and doesn't move. Pause.* KILBY *throws the leg down, goes over to* PADDY.

PADDY. Me leg's broke. Fuck. I know it. Agh!

> KILBY *takes the baseball bat off him.*

KILBY. Broke?

PADDY. I'm tellin' you.

KILBY. Well, there's another one.

> KILBY *whacks* PADDY*'s other leg with the bat.* PADDY *screams.*

. . . Keep it company.

> KILBY *sits down. Pause.* PADDY *moaning.*

Not too often that happens, Paddy. Tell you that. A hunch doesn't play for the Kilby? Bit disappointin' man. 'Cos you *couldn't* hack it, could you?

(*Touches* PADDY*'s leg with bat.*) Could you?

PADDY. Agh! No! No, I couldn't!

KILBY. . . . . After sayin' you could.

PADDY. I *thought* I could. (*Short pause.*) Unh. I *thought* I could.

KILBY. *I* thought so too, man. (*Pause.*) Fuck it. Faggots like yourself don't belong in the echelons, anyway. Weak willed fucks.

PADDY. I am.

KILBY. Huh . . . ?

PADDY. I *am* a weak willed fuck.

KILBY. Don't tell *me,* man. *Very* disappointed, I am. You coulda been the nik-nak kid, coulda been me 'prentice man. Two of us all buddy-buddy vicious, fuckin' *legends.* S'ppose I'm destined to journey solo, so, without partner or companion, alone in the echelon. S'ppose that's me fate, man. (*Pause.*) Still. 'Preciate the skullhallin'. Stopped me buggerin' Hughie at least. Could've got into trouble for that with Puppacat, fucked him up *too* bad there, denied Bernie his vengeance, you know? Could've set meself up for a disciplinin'. So thanks for that, man. Gratitude. (*Pause.*) Still an' all. Still have me rage horn . . .

PADDY. Your what?!

KILBY. . . . . between me legs. Me rage horn! Need to douse the flame, man, drain the blood from me cock 'fore Puppacat comes, clear me head an' calm me down for focused explainin'. Still too tumescent in me fury, I am. (*Short pause.*) You wanted to see me smashin' skills, Paddy? Me barehanded skills?

PADDY. Ah, no.

KILBY. Well, now you're gonna. Ah, no, I'll show you, now.

PADDY. Kilby.

KILBY. You ready? This'll bring back me balance.

PADDY. Kilby!

> KILBY *now on his knees, begins deep meditative breathing with arm movements, eyes shut, his breathing gets faster and faster, becomes more intense.* HUGHIE *has recovered consciousness. He gets up, picks up the baseball bat and approaches* KILBY *from behind.* KILBY*'s breathing, now louder, reaches a crescendo, his right hand raised for the fatal strike.* PADDY *repeats 'Kilby, Kilby', over and over, pleading.* KILBY *lets a final shout and* HUGHIE *smacks him viciously in the head with the bat. He topples over and is still. Pause.*

PADDY. Oh, Jesus! Oh, Jesus!

HUGHIE. You all right?

PADDY. Me fuckin' legs! (*Tries to get up without success. Lets out a shout of pain.*) Oh, fuck, man! *Fuck!* Fair *dues,* man!

Pause. HUGHIE *begins rushing around the apartment, packing clothes etc. into a bag. Continue 'til stated.*

Me fuckin' legs! Fuckin' *animal!* (*To* KILBY.) We got you, you *cunt,* you! We *slew* the goliath, (*To* HUGHIE.) Didn't we? Defeated him *wicked,* me fuckin' *leeegs*!!! (*Short pause.*) Agh . . . ! The fuck're you doin'? . . . *Je*sus!

HUGHIE. Splittin'.

PADDY. Off?

HUGHIE. . . . The fuck out of here, Paddy. Yeah. (*Pause.*)

PADDY. What about me, man? You givin' me a jockey?

HUGHIE. Sorry, man. Have to be nimble for me 'scape. You made your bed . . .

PADDY. Me legs!

HUGHIE. . . . Lie in it. Your what?

PADDY. I took wallops for you.

HUGHIE. An' thankful I am, Paddy. Saved me a brolly up me dirty dirt-road. I'm 'preciative. But you deserted me me hour of need, man. Sided 'gainst me, 'gainst me oul'one.

PADDY. Your oul'one?

HUGHIE. . . . Sided 'gainst us proper. Name's Dolly, man. She was buried today, 'case you forgot. (*Silence.*)

PADDY. I remember now . . . Hughie!

HUGHIE. What?

PADDY. What she said was . . .

HUGHIE. Oh, you *remember* now?!

PADDY. Yeah, it just came to me. We were in the sittin' room . . . Ah, shit! We'd, we'd hot whiskeys an' dry roasters, am I right?, peanuts, an' I started . . . I spilt my whiskey, started, cryin' 'cos of the stress of the day, man, the events that were in it. . . . started cryin' an' she hugged me, I remember, man, an' said it was okay. It was okay because she'd be . . . (*In pain.*) Agh!

HUGHIE. Go on.

PADDY. Don't know how I forgot. Said she'd be me mother . . .

HUGHIE. Yeah . . . ?

PADDY. . . . long as you were my brother. (*Pause.*) Isn't that it? Long as . . .

HUGHIE. No.

PADDY. No?! *Yes,* man!

HUGHIE. Long as you were mine, Paddy. Long as you were mine, an' as of today, man . . .

PADDY. You fuck!

HUGHIE. . . . you're Kilby's, aren't you. Tell *him* your problems.

PADDY. I can't. (*Pause.*) Hughie! (*Pause.*) The fuck am I supposed to do?

HUGHIE. Tell you what. If the cunt's no more, all right? If he's kicked, you can tell Puppacat it was me battered the pair of youse. Might get you off the hook if you're convincin'. But if he's alive, now . . .

PADDY. He'll tell them I helped you.

HUGHIE. That's right.

PADDY. They'll scalp me.

HUGHIE. That's right. Among *other* inventive shit. (*Long pause.*)

PADDY. Check for us.

HUGHIE. Hm?

PADDY. . . . If he's dead, man. Will you?

HUGHIE. Sorry, Paddy. Fugitive has to be scabby with his time, 'cos he's *got* none. Surely you can crawl that far. (*Puts on his jacket.*)

PADDY. You fuck!

HUGHIE. Well . . .

PADDY. . . . Why're you doin' this?

HUGHIE. . . . Somethin' I've learnt today, Paddy. (*Picks up bag and a can of lager, looks out window, then going to door.*) Somethin' you helped teach me.

PADDY. What's that?

HUGHIE. You *an'* the oul'one. (*Opens door, turns to* PADDY.) You do what's right for yourself, man.

PADDY. Hughie . . .

HUGHIE. . . . Long as you're able to hack it. That right?

PADDY. . . . Give us a jockey.

HUGHIE (*opens the can. Holds it up*). So here's to youse both. Can't, man.

PADDY. Hughie.

HUGHIE. . . . Or rather won't. (*Drinks the whole can.*) Aahh! (*Throws can in the corner.*) Adios, partner.

PADDY. Hughie!

The door shuts. HUGHIE *is gone.* PADDY *tries without success to get up. He lets out a shout of pain. Pause.* KILBY *groans.*

Oh, no . . . (KILBY *groans again.*) . . . no, fuck! Fuck! Fuck!

PADDY *crawls over to* KILBY, *very slowly, shouting in pain as he goes, sits beside him, picks up the baseball bat. He starts crying, stops abruptly, composes himself, looks at* KILBY. *Long pause. He raises the bat. Hold. Brings it down to his lap, begins weeping again as the lights fade down to darkness . . .*

The end.

A Nick Hern Book

Made in China first published in Great Britain in 2001
as a paperback original by Nick Hern Books, 14 Larden Road,
London W3 7ST, in association with the Abbey Theatre, Dublin

Made in China copyright © 2001 by Mark O'Rowe

Mark O'Rowe has asserted his right to be identified as
the author of this work

Typeset by Country Setting, Kingsdown, Kent, CT14 8ES

Printed and bound in Great Britain by Biddles of Guildford

ISBN 1 85459 627 6

A CIP catalogue is available from the British Library